The
Centered Life

Awakened   Called   Set Free   Nurtured

by Jack Fortin

Foreword by Richard Bliese

Augsburg Fortress

Centered Life
AN INITIATIVE OF LUTHER SEMINARY

*I would like to dedicate this book
to my loving wife and soul mate, Sara,
who has been the primary shaping influence
in my life and work.*

Large-quantity purchases or custom editions of this book are available at a discount from the publisher. For more information, contact the sales department at Augsburg Fortress, Publishers, 1-800-328-4648, or write to: Sales Director, Augsburg Fortress, Publishers, P. O. Box 1209, Minneapolis, MN 55440-1209.

Scripture passages are from the New Revised Standard Version of the Bible, copyright © 1946, 1952, 1971, 1989 by the Division of Christian Education of the National Council of the Churches of Christ in the USA. Used by permission.

Library of Congress Cataloging-in-Publication Data
Fortin, Jack, 1945-
  The centered life: awakened, called, set free, nurtured / by Jack Fortin; foreword by Richard H. Bliese.
    p. cm.
  Includes bibliographical references.
  ISBN 0-8066-5287-X (pbk. : alk. paper)
  1. Spiritual life—Christianity. 2. Christian life. I. Title.
  BV4501.3.F65 2005
  248.4—dc22   2005030370

Cover design by Laurie Ingram; cover photo © Royalty-Free/Corbis. Used by permission; book design by Michelle L. N. Cook

The paper used in this publication meets the minimum requirements of American National Standard for Information Sciences—Permanence of Paper for Printed Library Materials, ANSI Z329.48-1984. ♾™

Manufactured in the U.S.A.

10   09   08   07   06   1   2   3   4   5   6   7   8   9   10

Contents

Foreword by Richard Bliese   5

Chapter 1: Longing for a Centered Life   7

Chapter 2: Awakened to God's Presence   25

Chapter 3: Called to Life   45

Chapter 4: Set Free to Work with God   71

Chapter 5: Finding Nurture and Support   91
     for Living Out Your Callings

Notes   108

Recommended Reading   110

Acknowledgments   112

Foreword by Richard Bliese

If you sense that there is more to living the Christian life than constantly striving for a balanced lifestyle between all the various demands on you at work, home, in your community, and in your congregation, you've come to the right book. Jack Fortin leads us away from the myth of "the balanced life" to one that is centered in Christ. The shift from "balance" to "faithfulness" lies at the heart of this book's message. Discipleship, therefore, involves ministry in daily life. And ministry in daily life means making the important connection between Sunday and Monday.

This book represents a major commitment by Luther Seminary to teaching ministry in daily life. Jack Fortin, who has directed Luther Seminary's Centered Life Initiative since 2001, has led the charge to map out concrete ways in which the local congregation becomes the place where Christians not only discover their callings in the world but are equipped to fulfill them. Within a world of fragmentation, many feel that they are losing control. Christians long for answers and lives that count for something worthwhile, both inside and outside the walls of their congregations. They want to know what God is doing in the world and what their role in this plan is. The Centered Life Initiative at Luther Seminary in

St. Paul, Minnesota, provides a framework for change for congregations that strive to teach their people about their callings in daily life. Lutherans have lamented the fact for five hundred years that Luther's insights into the priesthood of all believers has been neglected by our congregations. Now is the time to do something about that. This book points the way forward.

The major emphases of the Reformation were twofold: justification by grace through faith, and vocation. A local congregational mission strategy that strives to be faithful and effective must build on both dynamics. Luther left his monastery and entered the world, thus starting a religious reformation. A major goal of this book is to address the unfinished reformation in American congregations. It is time for Christians in North America to leave their own monasteries as well. A new reformation awaits them.

Wonderful examples, anecdotes, concrete suggestions, and biblical directions fill every page concerning living a life of belonging, identity, and meaning centered in Christ. This is a book that you will want to read over and over again—and one that you will want to discuss with your friends and your small-group members.

Once you start reading this book in your congregation, watch out! God will use this book to initiate change. That is its purpose. The more centered in Christ we become, the more we are opened to God's mission in the world. Thanks be to God for Jack Fortin's commitment to call us all to lives centered in Christ.

—*Richard Bliese*
President, Luther Seminary
St. Paul, Minnesota

Chapter 1

Longing for a Centered Life

"I seem to be one person when I'm visiting my mother in the nursing home, another when I'm with my friends at the health club, still another at work, and someone else at church. Sometimes I have a hard time keeping all my separate selves straight. I feel like a chameleon. I wonder, Which one is the real me?"

"As a single mom, I feel torn to pieces by all the demands on my time. I try to do a good job at work and be a good parent to my kids and take care of my dad when he needs my help. I have no time for myself. I feel overwhelmed. I feel as if I don't do anything well. My life seems to be falling apart into a million pieces."

"I looked forward to retirement and thought it would be the best time of my life. But after a few months of golfing and a Caribbean cruise, I'm restless and bored. I still want my life to have some meaning. I'm not ready to give up on life yet."

"At work I'm being asked by my supervisors to do things that I think are quasi-moral and maybe even illegal, but

basically I like my job, and, frankly, I'm afraid of losing it. I'm not finding any moral guidance at church. The sermons and Bible studies never seem to have anything to do with the situations I'm facing. I'm not sure my pastor has any idea of the issues I face at work."

"I have two friends, both of whom are dedicated, committed Christians. One believes that being a Christian means opposing abortion, gay marriage, and gun control. She fully supports the war in Iraq. The other is for gay rights, peace, and the rights of immigrants. I admire both of them for their convictions but often I feel torn between them."

Voices like these, and many others, express what many people are feeling in our society: a loss of identity, fragmentation, meaninglessness, a loss of control, feeling alone, adrift without a moral compass, confused, anxious.

We long for a more centered life, a sense of wholeness, a more peaceful, confident life. We want a place to belong, and we want our lives to count for something worthwhile. The good news is that this is possible. It is possible to live a centered life. We are not meant to live divided and fragmented lives. God intends for us a life of wholeness, belonging, and meaning. This book will explore the process of moving toward a centered life.

Our Fragmented Lives

Although many of us yearn for a more centered life, we find it very difficult to get there. Why is it so hard? A first step is to understand some of the trends in our society that tend to pull our lives apart and leave us without a center.

The rapid pace of change. Daily life around 1800 was not much different from daily life in the time of Jesus. People traveled only as fast as a horse could run or a ship could sail. Messages traveled at the same speed. But beginning with the Industrial Revolution the lives of many people, at least in the industrialized nations, have experienced an increasingly rapid change of pace so that Alvin Toffler had to coin a new term, *future shock,* to describe this. Peter Vaill, professor of human systems at the University of St. Thomas, uses an image from canoeing to say that we are living in a "world of permanent white water."[1]

Closely related is the speeding up of the amount and the diversity of information that bombards us every day—through printed materials, radio and TV, computers, cell phones, and a host of new gadgets. To protect themselves from this information overload, people put up more "mental filters," so that while it used to be that someone had to hear a message eight times for it to soak in, now it takes twenty-seven repetitions.[2]

Mobility. Few of us live in one place for very long. We set down only shallow roots. Few of us work at one job for thirty or forty years. We no longer can trust corporations to provide us with a secure future. We no longer are surrounded by supportive friends and relatives. Among other things, this deprives us of a sense of accountability.

When I was a teenager, I worked at Johnny's Grocery Store in Rockford, Illinois, stocking shelves. I decided that I wasn't making enough money to buy my favorite potato chips, and I discovered that I could tuck one of those bags of chips inside my jacket on the way out of the store. I grew so successful at this that I started to shoplift larger and larger bags. Then one day as I was leaving, Johnny stopped me, unzipped my jacket, and the potato chips dropped out.

Because this was still a town where people had relationships with store owners, including a charge account, within ten minutes my parents were at the store talking with Johnny. For the next three months I was stocking shelves at no cost to Johnny. My father said, "Remember that when you cheat your neighbor, the cost is high."

In the search for the kind of community that used to exist more commonly, we are seeing a move from our big cities into smaller towns, where people can again know their neighbors and find security and support. There are also new suburban developments of "clustered housing" that seek to create the feeling of an old-fashioned neighborhood.

Specialization. As more and more low-skilled jobs are moved from the United States to Third World factories, the remaining jobs require highly skilled workers—specialists. Such specialization is necessary (I want my surgeon to be an expert at what he is doing), but it has a negative side. By giving myself over to a medical specialist, I may lose control and ownership of my own health care. Someone who performs only one specialized task in a project may lose the sense of the whole.

Diversity. Many of us grew up in towns or neighborhoods where everyone was basically like us. When I was a boy in Rockford, Illinois, there were basically two kinds of people—Swedes and Italians. The Swedes were Lutheran, and the Italians were Roman Catholic. And we thought that was diversity. Now even rural areas include people of diverse cultures and religions. Texas has now become the fourth state in which the "minorities" are a "majority," in which Caucasians are outnumbered by all others. (The other three states are California, New Mexico, and Hawaii.)

Our cities and towns and townships are no longer predominantly Christian. In many areas fewer and fewer people identify themselves as Christians or churchgoers. In North America and Europe, Christian culture seems to be in a decline, while in the southern hemisphere Christian churches are growing dramatically. We're living in a land with many cultures and religions—or with no religious background at all. Even within Christianity we tend to be divided or even polarized into factions.

Compartmentalization. Each of us lives in multiple communities, anywhere from four to seven. We may have one community that is our family, another our congregation, another our work, another our political party, still another a hobby or special interest group. Each of these communities has differing expectations and demands upon us. In each one we are known only in part. People yearn to bring their many selves together into one place where they can be whole and where they are known well.

Unrealistic expectations. We are driven by the message, "You can have it all if you just achieve the right balance." And so we run frantically from place to place, trying to have career, family, a rich social life, a gorgeous body, an influence in the community, a spiritual life.

Isolation. Driven in part by the proliferation of i-media, many of us find it easier and more convenient to interact with the world through electronic devices. Instead of joining other people in a movie theater, we watch a video or DVD in the privacy of our homes. We order our clothes online, perhaps even our groceries. Some "go to church" via radio, TV, or iPod. Instead of talking with a friend or colleague, we send an e-mail message. Some teenagers are reported to spend four hours a day exchanging text messages. Even within our homes we isolate ourselves from family members around our own TVs, our own computers, our own telephones.

These tools are by no means all bad. They offer us opportunities to keep in touch with people we might not communicate with otherwise. They offer us convenience and privacy, but they also result in a loss of community, of face-to-face contact with real people. For this reason some critics have strongly urged us to limit our use of these electronic media. One has called for a media sabbath, taking one day of the week without these electronic gadgets. When asked how we can find or create community, Minnesota writer Bill Holm, said, "Turn off the television and get to know your neighbors!"

A climate of fear. Bombarded with messages about terrorism, violence, crime, and financial crisis, we live in a culture of fear, described well by Lutheran Bishop Mark Hanson:

> Far too often, when fear becomes our orientation to the world, we either withdraw into isolation or resort to acts of aggression. Fear hardens lives and closes borders. Fear prevents us from being open to the radical newness of God's promises that call us to a life of faith.[3]

Church: The Solution or Part of the Problem?

Can we find a place that allows us to relate to a center, that helps us bring the diverse parts of our lives into some harmony? It is my conviction that the local congregation can be the place where this happens for us. Congregations are the best places for God's people to be inspired and equipped to live out their callings each day. In the congregation people can be led to find their center in God, as revealed in Jesus

Christ. At its best, the congregation can then offer us a safe place in which we can talk about the brokenness, fragmentation, and challenges of our daily lives, and where we can explore how to live our faith in every arena of our lives.

I recognize that too often the congregation does not do this. As I have heard from many people, they find little connection between Sunday worship and the everyday life of Monday and the rest of the week. At times the local congregation can even cause greater divisions for us by dividing us up into age groups or special interest groups or by giving us still more things to do. Church leaders reinforce the Sunday-to-Monday disconnect when they focus on internal maintenance, church growth, and programs instead of equipping people for work and ministry in God's world. The congregation then becomes yet one more competitor for our time.

But I believe it is possible to find support and guidance for a centered life in the congregation. The Centered Life Initiative at Luther Seminary in St. Paul provides a framework for change, seeking to ignite renewal in congregations, making them places where people gather, encounter Christ in word and sacrament, experience the support of Christian community, become equipped for everyday mission and ministry and then scattered to serve God in their many vocational settings.[4] We will explore that potential of congregational life further in chapter 5.

The Myth of the Balanced Life

Some social commentators have suggested that the answer to the divided life is a balanced life. Although they have some valuable things to say, I find that the balanced life is finally a myth; it can't be done. In a balanced life, I try to stay in control of my life and try to find ways to balance the various facets of my life: work, family, personal care, friendships, community life, and political involvement. The problem with this is that it keeps us self-absorbed, and the elements of our lives rarely stay in balance. Think of what happens, for example, when you have a sick child. Your goal then is not to maintain a balance, but to take immediate care of that child.

The alternative to a balanced life is a faithful life. It is a life faithful, moment by moment, to the God in whom we live and move and have our being. It is a centered life. The perfect example of the faithful life is Jesus Christ. Jesus often worked long hours despite the objections of his disciples, and at other times he withdrew from people and tended to his own needs for rest, reflection, and prayer.

Personal Exercise: How Centered Are You?

Take a few moments to reflect on your own life. To what extent is each of these statements true about you?

1. I regularly take time to reflect on God's work in my life.
2. I genuinely feel guided by God each day in the decisions I make.
3. Others can see my faith in action in the way I tackle daily tasks.
4. When things are tough for me, I get encouragement from other church members.
5. Knowing my own strengths helps me see how God has called me to serve others.
6. I see my work as a calling.
7. God created me with a unique pattern of strengths and talents.

8. Each day I am able to see how God is sending me out to do God's work.
9. I feel strongly connected to people in my church.

Christ: The Way to a Centered Life

We are not meant to live divided lives. We are made for wholeness and integrity.

God has placed within us a yearning to find a place where we experience a sense of belonging and make a difference in the world. This yearning raises questions:

- How do we know what we were created to be?
- How do we find those places where we can make a difference?
- Where can we experience a sense of belonging?

For Christians, the answers to these questions begin with God, the God who has created us, who has redeemed us, who dwells within us as power and presence. A life centered in the triune God gives identity and a place to stand in a chaotic and compartmentalized world. The Creator God is present in all I do. Christ is the example and provides the means for how I am to live and love in God's world. The Holy Spirit is the voice within me that guides the way I live.

With God as the center of my life, I know *whose* I am and can begin to discover *who* I am. I know what God created me to be. I have a prevailing sense of my unique pattern of strengths and use these strengths to create a more trustworthy world. Knowing my unique strengths helps me understand God's purposes and will for my life.

God calls us first to himself. We come to know God through Jesus Christ. We are found by God, and we find

God. Pastor Chris Bellefeuille of St. Barnabas Lutheran Church in Plymouth, Minnesota, said in a sermon, "Jesus seeks you out and finds you because you each have a unique role, a unique ministry in the kingdom. From the lowest, the least, and the lost to those who feel they might be on pretty firm footing, each of you is being sought. You have been forgiven and washed in grace so that you might be able to live as found people."[5]

From the beginnings of history—and before—God revealed himself to humankind through the creation (Romans 1) and through special people called prophets, but God revealed himself most clearly by becoming one of us in the person of Jesus Christ. "Long ago God spoke to our ancestors in many and various ways by the prophets, but in these last days he has spoken to us by a Son, whom he appointed heir of all things" (Hebrews 1:1-2). Now when we want to know who God is and what God is like, we have only to look to Jesus, who not only teaches us the truths of God but who embodies that truth. In his paraphrase of the New Testament, J. B. Phillips has this striking presentation: "Now Christ is the visible expression of the invisible God" (Colossians 1:15).

In this book I speak out of who I am, from my center as a Christian. At the same time I respect those of other faiths or no faith, as the apostle Peter learned, "that God shows no partiality, but in every nation anyone who fears him and does what is right is acceptable to him" (Acts 10:34-35). I believe I can help others most by being true to my own center.

In John 1:14 we read: "And the Word became flesh and lived among us, and we have seen his glory, the glory as of a father's only son, full of grace and truth." In and through Jesus we come to know the truths about God and ourselves and life, but also God's grace, God's unconditional acceptance of us apart from our achievements.

Referring to the biblical story, twentieth-century Lutheran preacher Edmund Steimle wrote:

> It's the story of living, sweating, rejoicing, struggling, dying men and women just like you, just like me. And the story tells of a God not apart from their daily ordinary lives, but smack in the middle of them. So it's my story too. And your story. Rejoice in it. Give thanks and sing. For the hope is not fanciful or ephemeral; it is rooted in a God who enters into the dirt and dust and joys of life precisely where you are now. Just like a child in the dust and dirt and joy of a stable.[6]

Faith is my saying "yes" to God's grace. A faithful centered life is my response to God's love and blessing.

Embodied Good News

Although I had heard the Christian gospel in my home and at my Methodist church, the gospel came alive for me when I was a teenager in Rockford, Illinois. I grew up in a family in which both parents were educators. My father grew up on a forty-acre farm in northwest Wisconsin. His father was a logger and consequently often absent from home. My father needed a friend outside the family. A Methodist preacher recognized my father's musical gifts and took him into his own home and helped him get a college education. My mother also assumed that the way to make a life was through education, but she grew up in a very nurturing family and brought that spirit of nurture into our family.

I knew that both my parents loved me, but I also felt that their approval was connected, at least in part, with my performing well.

The school system I was in was very competitive both in academics and in sports. It was very important for me to do well in school and to make a good showing in tennis and wrestling. In the classroom one of the most common test questions was "compare and contrast . . ." and I learned the lesson well—to compare my own life with everyone else's.

One problem with having your identity formed by comparing yourself with others is that after a while it is not enough to win; someone else has to lose. I had to feel good at the expense of someone else feeling bad. Another problem is that I can't get straight "A"s in everything; there is always someone else who's better.

I realized that in the fight for grades and for winning in sports, I confused approval or disapproval of my achievements with acceptance or rejection of my person, who I was.

I began to get a different message through a youth worker, a staff member of Young Life, named Bruce Sundberg, who began hanging out with me and my friends on the tennis court. For the first time we experienced an adult taking an interest in us, listening to us, without trying to change or control us. He won our allegiance, so much so that we even started to follow his example by wearing Hush Puppies.

Bruce did not let us make him a hero. He articulated to us in simple words the story of Jesus' death and resurrection and God's forgiveness. He said in effect, "I'm coming to you because I want to reflect a God who loves you more than I do and who will be with you when I am not."

Through Bruce I experienced God's unconditional love not just in words but embodied in a person. I came to believe that I was accepted because of God's grace and love and not because of what I did well. I had a sense of acceptance that set me free from an identity formed only by comparing myself with others.

In the community of faith there is the potential for discovering my value by virtue of my being a child of God through baptism. At Jesus' baptism God the Father declared, "You are my Son, the Beloved; with you I am well pleased" (Mark 1:11). I too can learn to hear God say, "You are my child. I love you, accept you, care for you unconditionally, apart from your achievements." But I also need to have this unconditional love embodied in persons in my life. And God has given me these gifts over and over in the course of my spiritual journey.

My Unique Center

Finding God, or having been found by God as I have come to know God in Christ, I can truly know myself. I know myself as a child of God, a creation of God. I am not God, but I have been created by God and for God. As Saint Augustine wrote in his spiritual autobiography: "You have made us for yourself, O God, and we are never at rest until we rest in you." The early twentieth-century spiritual writer Evelyn Underhill wrote:

> A spiritual life is simply a life in which all that we do comes from the centre, where we are anchored in God: a life soaked through and through by a sense of [divine] reality and claim, and self-given to the great movement of [God's] will.[7]

God created me with a unique set of gifts and potentials, as unique as my fingerprints. God gave me these gifts so that I can live a good life for myself and for others. When I have a realistic view of these gifts of God, neither denying them nor exaggerating them, I can operate out of a personal center, out of who I am, who I was meant to be.

Another aspect of my personal center is to understand my own ethnic and religious heritage. When I was on the staff of the Wilder Forest in Minnesota, a cross-cultural experiential education center, I was attempting to understand how to get people who come from different cultural settings and values to cocreate futures with people unlike themselves. At Wilder Forest we brought different cultures together by building villages with teenagers and their elders. In those villages the elders led the teenagers in rites of passage. We learned that if we helped young people find their cultural and spiritual roots, they would be more confident and open to work with people unlike themselves. We worked with each group to help them see and appreciate and appropriate what was unique about their culture. When they felt confident about their own cultural center, they were much less threatened by the "others."

At Wilder Forest I discovered that the deeper we understand and define ourselves by our center and not by our boundaries, the easier it is to work with people unlike us. We define ourselves by our boundaries when we look mainly at the barriers that separate us, at the ways we do things differently rather than at our core convictions.

Defining ourselves by our center is a way of inviting those different from us to tell their stories. Sometimes we make the mistake of looking only for what we hold in common. Unfortunately, we tend to get the lowest common denominator so low that no one has much interest in it, whereas, if we go deep within our own stories, we invite others to tell their stories. We then find that those different from us give shape and color to our stories without threatening our center.

Four Dimensions of a Centered Life

Early Christianity was called the Way. The centered life is also a way, not a one-time, one-size-fits-all conversion, but an ongoing process. I begin, I fall back, I gain greater clarity. I keep coming back to the process.

I understand the centered life for each one of us as a life of belonging, identity, and meaning centered in Christ that is:

- Awakened to God's presence in our life
- Called to live our faith in every situation
- Set free to contribute our unique gifts to God's work in the world
- Nurtured and supported by a community of faith.

It is important to understand that these four dimensions of a centered life do not happen in a strict time sequence. We do not first get awakened and then move on to being called, and so on. The dimensions are all interrelated, and we keep cycling through them according to our unique patterns of growth.

In the coming chapters we will explore together each of these four dimensions of the centered life.

Chapter 2 will describe some ways in which we become awakened to God's presence in our lives. We will see how

God often comes to us in unlikely people, unlikely places, unlikely events. We will search together to see how God is active in our everyday lives, as well as in church. We will share stories of how other people were awakened to God's presence and through this found support and meaning.

Chapter 3 will explore the questions: What should I do with my life? How does God call me? How can I live my faith in the four domains of the workplace, home, community, and congregation?

Chapter 4 will discuss how the gospel sets us free from the forces that hold us in bondage. In this chapter you will find ways of identifying your dependable strengths and your values and how to connect them with what God is doing in the world.

In chapter 5 you will discover ways to find the nurture and support you need for a centered life. A centered life is not a solo operation. If we try to go it alone, we end up in cynicism and burnout. We need the support of others. We will see how the church—in the form of the local congregation as well as other expressions of church—can assist. What can you expect from a congregation? What can you do if your congregation is not now providing that support? What kinds of spiritual practices can give strength to your daily life? Where else can you find or create the supportive network you need to live a centered, meaningful life?

Questions for Reflection and Discussion

1. Reread the voices at the beginning of the chapter. With which one do you most identify?

2. Of the reasons for our divided life, how does each one affect you?

Rapid pace of change Mobility
Specialization Diversity
Compartmentalization Unrealistic Expectations
Isolation Climate of fear

What other causes of uncentered life have you identified?

3. In what ways does your congregation help you lead a centered life? Are there any ways it contributes to the fragmentation of your life?

4. Can you identify a time when the gospel came alive in your life?

5. For me, Bruce Sundberg was one person who embodied the gracious love of God. Who have been the people who have done that for you?

6. What feels like the center of your life? How would your life be different if you more clearly had God as the center of your life?

7. Your personal center includes the gifts God has given you—your unique self. We will be exploring this idea further, in chapters 3 and 4, but for now, what do you see as your major God-given gifts and abilities?

8. What is your ethnic heritage? In what ways does it influence who you are and what you may uniquely contribute?

Chapter 2

Awakened to God's Presence

The great historian of religion Huston Smith said that in our time people are not satisfied only with doctrines about God or ethics about how to live. They are seeking an experience of God that transforms them. Like Job we cry out, "Oh, that I knew where I might find [God]" (Job 23:3).

Where do we find God? Some of our religious language and symbolism certainly can give the impression that God is somewhere else, "in heaven," somewhere in space far from our lives. Some people may limit the presence of God to a special holy place like a church and a worship service. Others may think of God as being in some beautiful favorite spot in nature, like a quiet lake surrounded by forest or an open prairie at sunset. All of these are true—God is transcendent, above and beyond anything we can think or experience. Yet God is also imminent, "closer to us than hands and feet" as one Christian writer declared. The apostle Paul used the words of a Greek poet to describe God's imminence: "He is not far from each one of us. For in [God] we live and move and have our being" (Acts 17:27-28).

God is in all those places, but we may need a larger picture of God. In his book *Your God Is Too Small*, J. B. Phillips wrote:

The trouble with many people today is that they have not found a God big enough for modern needs. . . . Many men and women today are living, often with some dissatisfaction, without any faith in God at all. This is not because they are particularly wicked or selfish or, as the old-fashioned would say, "godless," but because they have not found with their adult minds a God big enough to "account for" life, big enough to "fit in with" the new scientific age, big enough to command their highest admiration and respect, and consequently their willing cooperation.[1]

We need a big enough conception of God so we can recognize God's presence in unlikely places, indeed, in all of life. The problem often is not that God is absent from our lives, but that we are not awakened to God's presence. Theologian Marc Kolden writes:

The Christian doctrine of creation says that nothing exists with which God is not involved. The biblical understanding of creation tells us that in our daily life we have to do with God because God gives daily life and this earth and our neighbors and even our social structures. God gives these in part through human activity, but it is still God who gives all these things, according to the Bible.[2]

Kolden points out that Martin Luther recovered the biblical teaching of God's ongoing, ever-present creative work.

Not that God *controls* everything—humans are given a certain amount of freedom and responsibility for things on earth—but that since God gives all life, God is involved in some way in everything. As Luther portrays it, God's work is very concrete: God gives new babies through fathers and mothers; God raises children through parents, other family members, and teachers; God creates food through farmers and soil and sun and rain, and then through millers and butchers and processors, and distributors. Even if people don't realize it, they serve God as God works through them in their lives, relationships, and roles, using their activity and abilities to keep the world going and bless its inhabitants.[3]

Finding God in the Likely Places

We are guaranteed of finding God in the places where God has promised to be. One is in the word of God. God has promised to meet us through God's word, which we hear read and proclaimed in church, which we read in the Bible and other books of the Christian tradition, and which we hear from the mouths of fellow Christians.

Another place where God has promised to meet us is in the Sacraments of baptism and Holy Communion or the Lord's Supper. In baptism we hear again God's claim on us: "I have called you by name; you are mine." In Holy Communion we have Christ present with us "in, with, and under" the bread and wine.

In their book *Our Lives Are Not Our Own,* Rochelle Melander and Harold Eppley relate baptism to confirmation, a practice in many Christian denominations.

When we are confirmed, we affirm that our lives are not our own. We remember that when we were baptized, God claimed us as God's very own children: we were "sealed by the Holy Spirit and marked with the cross of Christ forever." When we were baptized, God said "yes" to us, an affirmation that resounds through every moment of our lives, in this world and the next.[4]

Confirmation is one of those places where we expect to meet God, even though for many young people this is still a time more of questioning than of affirmation of faith.

A Christian teacher was once asked: "How can I find God?" His answer: "Find some people who know God and be with them." In the fellowship of the church we find other believers who have been found by God and who continue to seek God.

But God is too great to be confined within the walls of a church building. God finds us, and we find God, in unlikely places.

Finding God in Unlikely Places

When I was in high school, I was dating a young woman I'll call Anne. At the time, her mother was dying of cancer. I decided, for reasons known only to a teenage boy, that it was time for me to break up with Anne. I didn't know how to do it gracefully, so with an extraordinary lack of social skills, even for me, I waited until one afternoon when I was standing with her at her bus stop. When her bus arrived, she stepped on, and just before the doors closed, I said, "I just wanted to tell you that I don't want to see you again."

That night Anne's mother died.

I was devastated. I felt tremendous remorse for the way I had treated Anne. I talked it over with my mother, who was very comforting.

At school, the situation was different. When the news got around school of how I had dumped Anne on the same day that her mother died, I was shunned by every other young woman at school and even by many of my friends. None of the teachers brought up the subject of the death of Anne's mother—or my poor judgment—except my civics teacher, who happened to be Jewish. She said to me privately, "I realize you're going through a lot of pain. I wonder if you feel as isolated as I sometimes do. I want you to know that you are a valuable person, even though your behavior has led to a sense of real isolation. If you ever want to talk about it, I'll be very willing to listen."

Never before had a teacher expressed such a personal interest in me. This awakened in me a sense of hope. I don't remember if I realized it at the time, but I now believe that it was God active and present in my life at this moment— not through my Christian teachers, but through this faithful Jewish woman.

One time the patriarch Jacob was isolated, on the run from his brother Esau whom he had cheated out of his inheritance. As he slept one night in the desert, he saw a vision of a ladder leading to heaven, and angels moving up and down the ladder. When he awoke, Jacob said, "Surely the LORD is in this place—and I did not know it!" (Genesis 28:16). For Jacob it was a moment of being awakened to God's presence in a strange, unlikely place.

Hearing the Still Small Voice

The prophet Elijah, fleeing for his life from the rogue queen Jezebel, came to the mount of God at Horeb. There Elijah waited to meet God. "Now there was a great wind, so strong that it was splitting mountains and breaking rocks in pieces before the LORD, but the LORD was not in the wind; and after the wind an earthquake, but the LORD was not in the earthquake; and after the earthquake a fire, but the LORD was not in the fire; and after the fire a sound of sheer silence" (1 Kings 19:11-12). In that silence Elijah heard the "still small voice" of God. We too need practice in waking up and hearing that still small voice of God.

We hear that voice of God in the Bible, the written word of God, as we hear it read and proclaimed in church, as we participate in the liturgy, and as we receive the Sacraments of baptism and Holy Communion. We hear that word through brothers and sisters in the faith.

Many of us have had the experience that suddenly one day, a phrase in the liturgy, a line of a hymn, something said in the sermon, comes alive for us by the power of the Holy Spirit, and we are awakened to a new insight, new direction, new hope, and comfort.

Being awakened to God's presence in our lives is a gradual process. It does not happen all at once, but through a series of fresh insights, new and deeper experiences of God's grace and truth.

On the Way

We can see this in the life of Jesus' disciples. I always find comfort in the fact that the disciples, even though they were present with Jesus every day, were so slow to catch on to what he was about or to the meaning of his words. We see that in a section of Mark's Gospel, chapters 8 to 10, sometimes titled "On the Way." As the disciples traveled with Jesus toward Jerusalem, he tried several times to explain to them that he was going to Jerusalem to suffer and die, but the disciples weren't able to accept that, because that was not the way they were expecting God's Messiah to act. They were looking for God to act by providing a powerful rebel leader, someone who would use military might to overthrow the hated Roman army of occupation. But Jesus had to awaken them to the strange idea: "See, we are going up to Jerusalem, and the Son of Man will be handed over to the chief priests and the scribes, and they will condemn him to death; then they will hand him over to the Gentiles; they will mock him, and spit upon him, and flog him, and kill him; and after three days he will rise again" (Mark 10:33-34).

The ultimate sign of God's presence would not be in a triumphant military campaign, but in capture, torture, an execution on a cross—and then a resurrection to new life.

Jesus was teaching the disciples to know him better, to know the Caller who had chosen them and called them to follow him. They came to know him slowly, step by step, and then not really until his resurrection.

They not only were slow to know the Caller, but they had to overcome a major misunderstanding about their call to follow him. Even after Jesus had given them a clearer and clearer picture of his coming suffering and death, Mark tells us that the disciples "did not understand what he was saying and were afraid to ask him" (Mark 9:32).

Then after Jesus and his followers had traveled to Capernaum, Jesus asked them, "What were you arguing about on the way?" They seem to have been ashamed to tell him that they had been arguing about which of them would be the greatest in his coming kingdom.

Jesus tried to awaken them to a new understanding of what it meant to be his disciples: "Whoever wants to be first must be last of all and servant of all" (Mark 9:35). To make his point more clear Jesus placed a little child among them and said, "Whoever welcomes one such child in my name welcomes me, and whoever welcomes me welcomes not me but the one who sent me." Jesus was awakening them to the ideal that they were free not for a life of competition but for a life of service to others.

The Practice of Seeing

Martin Luther distinguished between a theology of glory and a theology of the cross. In a theology of glory God's presence is experienced only through the highs of life, the peak experiences like a dramatic healing, a phenomenal success, a dramatic supernatural experience. Although a theology of the cross does not deny that such "highs" sometimes happen to some people, it declares that the more common way to experience God is through the ordinary, natural events of everyday life. More than that, a theology of the cross even says that we may experience God most clearly in the "lows" of life, the brokenness and failures, even the zero point at which we are helpless to do anything for ourselves. As the apostle Paul wrote, "Whenever I am weak, then I am strong" (2 Corinthians 12:10).

When our lives are calm and stable, we may be oblivious to the presence of God. Often we are awakened in a time of crisis. The psychologist M. Scott Peck says that in times of stability, our life is like a triangle that is sitting firmly on its base. But in a crisis, our triangle is turned upside down, resting shakily on its point. Then it is easily moved and tipped. Adolescence is for most people such a period of crisis, so it is no wonder that many religious awakenings come to people during their teenage years.

When I was forty years old, I reached a true zero point in my life. I had been leading a very active, productive life as vice president of Young Life, working in nine states, when suddenly my life was brought to a standstill. I was skiing in Colorado, and two days later I was in a wheelchair being wheeled through the Denver airport and helped onto a plane. By the time I reached the airport in my hometown of Madison, Wisconsin, my legs felt as if they were completely dead. I crawled out of the plane on my hands and knees.

I was taken to the hospital, where my family doctor examined me and after fifteen minutes said, "I'm 96 percent sure that what you have is Guillain-Barré syndrome [a disorder of the immune system that attacks the myelin sheathing of the nerves and leads to paralysis]. What I can promise you is that I will keep you alive, and that one day you'll be able to walk again, because this does reverse itself. But that's all I'll guarantee you. Tomorrow morning you might be blind or on a respirator. We don't know where this disease will take you, but for the next twenty-one days your body will break down, and after that it will start to rebuild. If we can turn it around sooner, you have a greater chance of full recovery."

Suddenly, here I was, an aggressive, competitive, white male of northern European heritage, and I'd become a vegetable. It took two nurses to lift me from the bottom of the bed to the top.

In my distressing state of helplessness, a neuropsychiatrist was sent to talk with me. He was a divorced Jew who did not practice his faith. He was dressed in flashy clothes and drove a red BMW convertible. He came three times a week and sat there with me. He was not the person I looked to for help.

One day I was in a group session with other paralyzed patients in which a pastor lectured us about hope. I was so frustrated by this that I raised my hand and said, "Why are you giving us an intellectual lecture on hope? We need to hear something that will give us hope, that will give us a reason to keep on."

I turned to the man next to me, a big old Irishman named Charlie McCarthy, and said, "Charlie, wouldn't it be great if we could believe in a God who somehow loved us for who we are and who would come and give us some clear promise of help?"

"You're right about that!" Charlie replied. "I wish there was someone like that out there."

I was wheeled back to my room crying, totally discouraged. In walked the neuropsychiatrist. He said, "You don't like me do you? You don't like anything about me, but that's okay, because I didn't come here because I need your affirmation. But I do have something to say to you. I hear you are a pastor, a person of faith. The doctors and nurses have done everything they can do, and now they're waiting for God to heal you. Why can't you wait for God to heal you?" He left, slamming the door behind him.

It was what I needed. It awakened me to my false need to control my own healing rather than to let God heal me. At times we limit God's activity through our own expectations of how we think God's help will come to us, but God breaks into our lives in mysterious and unlikely ways.

Awakened by a Prayer Overheard

Steven was a successful surgeon in the Los Angeles area. His teenage daughters were involved in a youth group that I led. When I first met Steven, he would hardly speak to me, but over time he and I became friends as he saw the positive effects of the youth group on his daughters.

Unfortunately, Steven had something of a know-it-all attitude that was off-putting to many people. He was an outstanding surgeon but lacked bedside manners with his patients. He once said of his patients, "I like them best when they are on the operating table unconscious." This aloof attitude carried over into a strained relationship with his daughters and, I think, added pressure on Steven's wife to be the go-between for Steven and his daughters.

I learned that one night, as Steven was heading to bed, he passed by his daughters' bedroom and overheard his name being mentioned. The door to the bedroom was slightly ajar, which caused him to pause. He heard one of his daughters praying. In the prayer she was admitting how much she loved and admired her father but went on to lament how inadequate her relationship with her father was, how he was at times insensitive to her and others, and how much she hoped that God could wake him up and help him be more loving to her and the other children in the family.

Steven, as he told me later, was shocked at the revelation and frustrated that he had no way to talk about this with his daughters because he had been eavesdropping. He did not sleep well that night, woke early, and immediately called me and asked that we have breakfast that morning.

When we met, he reviewed with me what had happened and asked me what I thought. "Well," I said, "does it come as a surprise to you that others see you the same way? People respect your ability as a surgeon but do not experience you as a sensitive loving person. I'm afraid that sometimes you come off as arrogant and self-centered."

Steven looked at me in surprise. He was quiet, and I saw hurt in his eyes. I'm not sure why he responded so uncharacteristically at that particular moment. Perhaps we are all especially vulnerable when it comes to our children. I think that was true for Steven, but I also think he was at a time in his life and career when he had achieved success and prominence and now these achievements did not fill the void of meaning and belonging in his life. I think it was also the prompting of God's spirit in Steven, calling him to more in life than he had experienced in his self-made, self-controlled world. Indeed it was a rekindling of faith for Steven and with that was new motivation to live life differently.

We figured out a way for Steven to talk with his daughters and ask for their forgiveness—a major step for Steven. He also decided to work on his relationship with his patients and asked that I help him with his bedside manner. For several weeks I went into the operating room and stood next to Steven and prayed for his patients as he did surgery. I would then follow him in his rounds and give him feedback on his bedside manner, helping to develop more effective listening and affirming skills.

After some months Steven decided that he would cut back on the number of surgeries he was doing and spend time with young people, teaching them how to play tennis, a sport that Steven played well and enjoyed.

Other people in the community wondered why I was spending so much time with Steven and would imply that I was wasting my time: "He isn't going to change. And furthermore he is too busy to ever be involved in your ministry with youth." But they were wrong. I saw how God's spirit transformed Steven to become an open and more broken person who discovered God at work in his job, in his home with his children, and in his community involvement in helping kids learn a sport that was life-giving to him. He even slowed his practice down to the point of successfully running for the school board and has since established a consultancy for helping kids develop positive attitudes toward learning. Here is an amazing example of an ordinary person being drawn by the love of God into seeing all that he did with his life as a response to God's grace in his life.

The unlikely experience of overhearing his daughter's prayer led to real personal transformation for Steven. It was not simply a private benefit for him; his awakening led to him to be a blessing to the entire community. I firmly believe that our faith is deeply personal but not private. The deep intimacy that God desires for us leads us to have the power and mission to serve our neighbor, and draws us to others in a community of faith where we can be nurtured and supported.

I hope that my story and the story of Steven will enkindle in you your own stories. It's in our stories that we begin to learn about each other and we discover with one another what God is doing.

Awakening to God's Presence

How can you learn to be more aware of God's presence in all of your life?

We begin with our hearing and reading of God's word in the Bible. We know how God acts in our lives by seeing clearly how God has acted in the past.

Secondly, it's a matter of having an attitude of expectancy. We see what we expect to see. Maybe that's why the Bible encourages us to "Wake up!" as in the letter to the

Ephesians: "Sleeper, awake! Rise from the dead, and Christ will shine on you!" (Ephesians 5:14). The apostle Paul had a strong sense of urgency about this need for spiritual alertness. "You know what time it is, how it is now the moment for you to wake from sleep. For salvation is nearer to us now than when we became believers; the night is far gone, the day is near" (Romans 13:11-12).

Thirdly, we can pray for awakening. When Jesus was "on the way" with his disciples, near the city of Jericho, they came upon a blind beggar named Bartimaeus. When this blind man heard that Jesus was passing by, he called out several times, "Jesus, Son of David, have mercy on me!" Jesus called Bartimaeus to come to him and asked him, "What do you want me to do for you?" (Mark 10:51). The blind man replied, "My teacher, let me see again."

The prayer of Bartimaeus can be ours too. "Divine Teacher, let me see again. Open my eyes to your presence in my life, in all the ways that you come to me, even through unlikely people and unlikely events in unlikely places."

We do not gain this insight all at once, but in many small touches. Another time in Jesus' ministry he encountered a blind man at Bethsaida:

[Jesus] took the blind man by the hand and led him out of the village; and when he had put saliva on his eyes and laid his hands on him, he asked him, "Can you see anything?" And the man looked up and said, "I can see people, but they look like trees, walking." Then Jesus laid his hands on his eyes again; and he looked intently and his sight was restored, and he saw everything clearly. (Mark 8: 22-25)

God deals with each of us as individuals, providing the awakenings as we need them and according to our ability to receive them.

Often it is only in retrospect that we understand what God has been doing in our lives. A famous philosopher wrote that life is lived forward, but understood backward.

Fourthly, we are aided in our awakening by being in a community of faith. When our own vision is darkened, others may help us see what is going on. Other believers who have learned to listen for the still small voice of God can help you discern the sometimes subtle and ambiguous call of God in your life.

We need a safe place, what someone has called a "holding environment," in which we can give voice to our confusion and hurt and find empathetic and wise listeners. A small group in a congregation can be that kind of "holding environment."

Fifthly, we need practice waiting for God. The best discussion I know in our need to wait for God is in "A Spirituality of Waiting: Being Alert for God's Presence in Our Lives" by the Roman Catholic spiritual writer Henri Nouwen.[5] "Most people consider waiting a waste of time," he says. "Perhaps this is because the culture in which we live is basically saying, 'Get going! Do something! Show you are able to make a difference! Don't just sit there and wait!'" In addition to the feeling that we need to make something happen, we are fearful of our inner feelings, other people, the future. We need to hear God's word: "Be not afraid."

Waiting is never a movement from nothing to something, Nouwen says. "It is always a movement from something to something more." And waiting is not passive but active.

The secret of waiting is the faith that the seed has been planted, that something has begun. Active waiting means to be present fully to the moment, in the conviction that something is happening where you are and that you want to be present to it. A waiting person is someone who is present to the moment, who believes that this moment is the moment.

According to Nouwen, waiting is open-ended.

Open-ended waiting is hard for us because we tend to wait for something very concrete, for something that we wish to have. . . . Our waiting is a way of controlling the future. We want the future to go in a very specific direction, and if this does not happen, we are disappointed and can even slip into despair.[6]

That is certainly what happened to me in the worst of my struggles with Guillain-Barré disease. God was at work in me, teaching me to wait open-endedly.

Nouwen again:

To wait open-endedly is an enormously radical attitude toward life. So is the truth that something will happen to us that is far beyond our own imaginings. So, too, is giving up control over our future and letting God define our life, trusting that God molds us according to God's love and not according to our fear. The spiritual life is a life in which we wait, actively present to the moment, trusting that new things will happen to us, new things that are far beyond our own imagination, fantasy or prediction.[7]

Here again we need the support of a "holding community," a group of faithful believers who can support us when we find it hard to wait, when our own trust in God's love grows feeble, when we need the faith of others.

Awakened to Grace

Many in our society experience life as meaningless, fragmented, compartmentalized, isolated, anxious. There is an answer to this based on two key ideas from the Christian tradition, expressed clearly in the work of the church reformers of the sixteenth century, like Martin Luther. These "twin pillars" of the Reformation are the doctrines of grace and of vocation.

The first pillar of the Reformation is the doctrine of grace, the note sounded by Martin Luther, John Calvin, and their colleagues of the biblical doctrine stated in Ephesians: "For by grace you have been saved through faith, and this is not your own doing; it is the gift of God—not the result of works, so that no one may boast" (Ephesians 2:8-9). According to this central tenet, shared by Christians throughout the world, is the idea that we do not go out in search of God; God is searching for us. God calls us in love to be in a living relationship with God. We are called to Someone, not to something.

One of my favorite biblical promises about God's call is in Isaiah 43:

> But now thus says the Lord, he who created you, O Jacob, he who formed you, O Israel: Do not fear, for I have redeemed you; I have called you by name, you are mine. When you pass through the waters, I will be with you; and through the rivers, they shall not overwhelm you;

when you walk through fire you shall not be burned,
and the flame shall not consume you. (43:1-2)

In these verses "Jacob" and "Israel" refers to an individual, but also to the whole people of Israel. We experience God's call to us as personal, but it also comes to us in community.

God continues to call us through the church, through word and sacrament. There we experience the good news that our salvation comes from God; it is not our own doing.

The German theologian Eberhard Jüengel wrote in *Justification: The Heart of the Christian Faith:*

> For believers know that since God has done enough
> for our salvation, we can never do enough good for the
> world. So we are justified by faith alone, but faith never
> stays alone; it strives to, it has to become active in love;
> faith is never alone. There is no more liberating basis
> for ethics than the doctrine of justification of sinners
> by faith alone.[8]

At certain times and places in the Christian church the grace of God has been mistakenly limited to the issue of guilt and forgiveness. Grace then is seen only as a rescue from this earth, the means whereby we "get to heaven when we die." But God's grace is much larger than the matter of sin and guilt. Lutheran theologian Joseph Sittler wrote:

> The grace of God is not simply a holy hypodermic
> whereby my sins are forgiven. It is the whole giftedness
> of life, the wonder of life, which causes me to ask ques-
> tions that transcend the moment.[9]

Among those questions are two that are basic to the lives of each one of us: Where do I belong? Where can I make a difference? In grace God calls us to join in God's creative work here in the world, in "down-to-earth" ways.

As we awaken to God's saving, guiding, empowering presence, we are able to recognize what God is calling us to do with our lives. We will explore the topic of God's calling in the chapter that follows.

Questions for Reflection and Discussion

1. How would you explain your concept of God to a bright ten-year-old?

2. Where do you see God active in your daily life?

3. What are the "likely places" where you expect to encounter God?

4. In what unlikely events, persons, or places have you experienced God's presence?

5. What can you learn from the "on the way" stories of Jesus' disciples?

6. How have you experienced God in a "zero point" event or situation in your life?

7. Of the suggestions for "Awakening to God's Presence," which seem more significant for your life?

8. What have you learned about grace—"the first pillar of the Reformation"?

Chapter 3

Called to Life

With God as our center we live in unconditional love. Freed from the need to earn our salvation or justify our existence on earth, we ask, "Now what? Now what is my life for?" The Christian answer is: God's grace frees you to love and serve your neighbor. You are free to become a "little Christ" to the people in your life, your community, God's world.

God Calls Us in and into the World

This call to serve the neighbor as a "little Christ" is the second pillar of Reformation Christianity, the doctrine of vocation or calling.

Luther Seminary professor James Nestingen has written:

> The doctrine of vocation properly follows as a necessary partner of justification. Restoring the creature to the creation, as part of the larger act of retrieving the earth from the thrall of those powers that have demeaned and destroyed it, the risen Christ calls his own into the life-bestowing, creation-sustaining

vocations of everyday life. Instead of treating us as interchangeable parts caught accidentally in various patterns of relationship, he makes us in our own time and place, indispensable partners in the shaping of those with whom we share life, in the family, at work, in the larger community, and in the church.[1]

In a 1993 statement the Evangelical Lutheran Church in America declared:

God calls all Christians to a life of vocation. To have a "vocation" means to live out one's call. For Christians, that call is answered in the structures of daily life—family, work, state, service to the neighbor, care of creation—as the setting in which to live out their identity in the gospel.[2]

At the time of Luther the idea was prevalent that being a "real" Christian means that you were called out of the world, into a monastery to serve God there through prayer, or through being a priest or bishop in the church. Still today, many have the idea that only ministers or pastors are called, and their call is to full-time work in the church.

Luther stated clearly that all Christians have a vocation or calling from God and all are equal before God. The Christian's call or vocation is not limited to a paid job but is about any work we do in the world, in fact. We can think of it as happening in four domains: workplace, home, community, and congregation.[3]

Called in the Workplace

It is possible to think of work as anything in which we are vested. Work in this sense would include unpaid work at home or in the congregation or community. But for the purpose of our discussion here we will use the term *workplace* as defined by Paul Minus in *Taking Faith to Work:*

> From the perspective of Christian faith, our workplace is wherever we spend a significant portion of our time, engaged in activity (whether compensated or not) that produces goods and services, that makes use of our God-given talents, and that provides us an opportunity to serve God's purposes in the world.[4]

Harvard Business School researcher Laura Nash and Scotty McLennan, dean for religious life at Stanford University, coauthored a book called *Church on Sunday, Work on Monday: The Challenge of Fusing Christian Values with Business Life.* In discussing the problem of the Sunday-Monday disconnect, they write:

> No doubt about it. There has been a sea change in the way business people are approaching the problems of business and work. Spirituality, however defined, is now a popular resource for business needs, whether for sparking creativity, or for being a better person on the job. Run a search on the Internet for business and spirituality and fifteen hundred Web sites will pop up. Some form of spiritual practice can be found in most business settings today. People meditating at their desks, calling on faith to help them stay the course during hard times, silently calling on angels, acting out a faith-based compassion, or simply striving for a Buddha-like mindfulness.[5]

Sadly, many people are not looking to a Christian congregation for help in connecting their work and their spirituality, although there are many Christian themes that can help us make the Sunday-Monday connection in the workplace.

God calls us in our work in individual ways that fit our own unique personalities and situations. Let's look at the stories of two encounters of individuals with Jesus: Simon the fisherman (later renamed Peter) and Zacchaeus the tax collector.

Simon Peter was busy working with his partners James and John, washing his nets along the lake of Gennesaret (Luke 5:1-11). Jesus was preaching to a crowd of people who pressured him so much that he asked Peter to take his boat out a short way into the lake, where Jesus could sit down in the boat and teach. When he finished teaching, Jesus said to Peter: "Put out into the deep water and let down your nets for a catch." Peter objected that they had fished all night and caught nothing. But something about Jesus impressed Peter enough so he followed Jesus' orders. And the results were amazing—so many fish were caught that Peter's nets were full to the bursting point. Jesus gave Peter a new call: "Do not be afraid; from now on you will be catching people."

It is significant that Jesus met Peter not in the synagogue but in the midst of his daily work. Jesus encountered Peter on the job and called him to a new kind of work—to be with Jesus in the two or three years of his active ministry of preaching, teaching, and healing.

We don't know if during that time Peter did any fishing, but we do know that after Jesus' death and resurrection, Jesus again found him fishing and Peter recognized Jesus and said, "It is the Lord." (John 21:1-14).

Zacchaeus had an occupation that was among the most detested in first-century Israel—being a tax collector for the hated Roman occupation forces. Tax collectors had a reputation for dishonesty, for becoming rich by "ripping off" the poor. He must have heard something about Jesus that intrigued him so much that he climbed up in a tree to get a better look at this wandering preacher (Luke 19:1-10).

As Jesus passed by, he called up to Zacchaeus and invited himself to the tax collector's home. The crowds on the street must have been amazed that Jesus would enter the home of a man in such a dishonorable profession.

As a result of his being with Jesus, Zacchaeus was transformed. He decided to give half of his wealth to the poor and to offer restitution to any people he had cheated. It is significant that Zacchaeus did not stop being a tax collector. Jesus did not call him to a different job. Zacchaeus was not called to a different life, but to live life differently—in his case with a generous eye for the poor and victimized.

Callings come in one of two ways. Sometimes it happens when we get an idea, we change everything in our lives, and we go in a whole new direction. But more often, calling isn't about *a different life,* but *living life differently* because of God's presence in our lives.

Dan owned and operated a barber shop. He was my barber, in part, because I was a youth worker at the time, and most of the male adolescents with whom I was working went to Dan and thought he was really cool—and for good reason. In many ways, Dan never grew out of adolescence himself. His barber shop was in an old house that Dan had fixed up into a retro 1950s atmosphere. (This was during the late 1960s and early 1970s.) He wore jeans to work, drove a late model Corvette, and simply loved young people.

As I got to know Dan, it became apparent through the many conversations we had while he was cutting my hair that he was restless. He was asking the question "Is this all there is to life?" On the surface, it appeared to me that he had all the success and security anyone could ask for. He had a loving wife, two delightful young boys, a dog, and all the toys any reasonable male adult of thirty-five could ask for!

One of my clues to his unrest and searching was the way he expressed interest in what I was doing with kids. He would comment that I was doing the most important thing in the entire world, being there for kids, helping to articulate God's presence in their lives by living in their day-to-day world. He would compare what he did with them and suggest that I was doing something really meaningful but he was "just cutting their hair."

One of the times when I was in getting a haircut, I asked him if he wished he were doing more than "just cutting hair." He replied, "Oh yeah, but I'm not sure where I am with God myself, and besides, cutting hair is what I do best." He did not want to change his lifestyle or workplace to do something different.

I asked him about his own boys and his relationship to them. Did he like how his relationship with them was going? Did he like to spend time with them just hanging out? He said he felt that he was a responsible parent seeing to it that his wife and kids got off to church each Sunday.

"What do you mean, seeing to it that they go to church?" I asked. "Don't you go with them?"

"Not really. I'm usually somewhat hung over from the night before and need to sleep while they are at church."

That was all to our conversation until a few weeks later when I received a startling call from Dan. He exclaimed with great emotion, "I want to talk with you. I think I have been converted."

"What happened?" I asked.

"Well," he said. "I was lying on the couch last Sunday watching a TV evangelist while recuperating from the previous night's party, just to see what he might say. All of a sudden for some unknown reason I found myself down on all fours in front of the TV praying a prayer of invitation, asking Christ to come into my life. You see, I was just lying there sort of listening to him and daydreaming when I heard him say something that sounded as though he were talking directly to me. He said, 'I know that some of you in the viewing audience are, right now, lying on your couch having sent your wife and kids off to church recovering from last night's party with a hangover, feeling miserable, guilty, unfulfilled, restless, and lonely. Now, listen to me,' he said, 'and get off of your couch and get down on the floor and put your face close to mine and pray this prayer so that you can get healed, forgiven, and restored by God's love.'

"Well," Dan said, "that was exactly how I was feeling and so I did exactly what he said. I prayed and then felt a sense of peace and well-being that I had never experienced before. Now I'm inspired to do things and live differently!"

I was at once both grateful for his newfound grace and disappointed that it was a TV evangelist who had reached him. I would have preferred that this had happened on a church retreat, but then, I also realized that my congregation probably was not going to reach Dan, given his background and interests. It was a humbling moment to realize that my job was to accept his experience and support Dan in his efforts to make the changes he wanted to make in his new life in Christ.

Like so many of us, Dan thought that God's calling on his life to mean he had to quit what he was doing and give his life to "full-time service." As we talked about his work as a barber, I asked him what difference God's presence and acceptance in his life could mean for his current work as a barber to young people. We explored ways in which Dan could begin to see his barbering not as an end in itself but rather a means to relating his faith to his daily work. In fact, could his daily work be the context for his ministry?

It dawned on Dan that while cutting hair he had about fifteen minutes to talk to young people about their life and dreams, fears and hopes. He could be a listener to his clients and provide a safe place for each person to feel accepted and valued. For Dan, a second conversion took place, a conversion to seeing his ordinary work as a calling, doing what he did best and loved most in the service of God's kingdom!

Dan was like the blind man in Mark 8 who needed a second touch by Jesus to really see. We are all like Dan needing a second touch of insight into God's intentions for us as not only loved of God but also given the strengths and abilities to experience the fulfillment that comes from allowing "our deep gladness to meet the world's deep need," to use an expression of Frederick Buechner.[6] In Dan's case, this meant giving young people a safe place to be themselves, to experience someone serving them by cutting their hair, conveying dignity to their lives and creating with God a more trustworthy world.

As time went on, Dan found ways and places to share his faith verbally as well, particularly as he got to know some of his young friends through his church involvement and through Young Life. But he was first and foremost set free to serve God by cutting hair.

James Nestingen relates vocation or calling to love of those around us:

> Whether it involves the household or requires movements beyond it into the community, a person's job specifies the location and shape of love of the neighbor. Whether it is changing a diaper, tending the sick, working in a field, teaching a class, or some other form of service, the job is another point of partnership between Creator and creature for the sake of the creation. The new Eve or Adam which comes forth in Christ Jesus, takes shape not over and above the ordinary, but deep down in the contrariness and complications of the everyday. So work is a vocation, an office or station which by its very character calls the sinner out of the self to be of some earthly good.[7]

In *Taking Faith to Work,* Paul Minus outlines four ways in which Christians are called in their workplace:

> *A ministry of competence:* serving God and neighbor by doing our work well, through full use of the gifts God has given each of us, so that the human family is built up and moved nearer the abundant life of the kingdom.
>
> *A ministry of caring:* being attentive and responsive to the needs and hurts of people in our workplace, so that they experience something of the authentic community God intends for the human family.
>
> *A ministry of ethics:* moving perceptions and practices of right and wrong at work to a higher level, so that workplace ethics better approximate the ways God wills people to live together.

A ministry of change: developing new institutional practices and systems that help all people be and do their best, so that the place of work more nearly becomes a place of grace.[8]

Called in the Home

When we speak of home as one of the domains, we are thinking of family in a very wide sense. In a sense we all have a home and a family. It can be our family of origin and include parents and grandparents, aunt and uncles, nephews and nieces. For some, *family* means spouse and perhaps children. Those without relatives nearby can think of our "family of choice," the network of friends that serve the role for us that family has served for many in the past.

James Nestingen has written about the various "offices" or roles in the family:

> [T]he family is all-encompassing. Every member holds an office, whether that of son or daughter, brother or sister, uncle, aunt, or grandparent. Those who for one reason or another don't assume the office of husband or wife still function in the other offices. . . . The family offices are all shaped in such a way that they each contribute to the overall well-being of the household. So, for example, uncles and aunts serve a particularly important function. They are close enough to parents to know firsthand both their gifts and limits; close enough to children to share in their development without having to assume all of the parental responsibilities. In this way, they provide important footing as children move out of the family into the community. Likewise grandparents, even if only by their aging and dying,

mark out the passages of life, and so condition their grandchildren's expectations.[9]

The home is a place for worship. For Luther, the family was the place in which Christian truths were to be taught. Our homes can become places of prayer, whether we worship with others in a small group or engage in our personal spiritual practices.

The home is also a place of service, a place in which we are called to express the love of God by caring and nurturing one another. For those who are married, this involves especially a faithful nurturing of the marriage relationship. Where there are children, a major form of caring is in the responsible rearing of children. For all, married and single, our homes can be places of hospitality, where friends and family can experience a safe and pleasant sanctuary.

The home is a place where we practice good stewardship of the things God has given us. Here too we can care for God's earth by sound environmental practices.

Luther had a very high view of the importance of marriage being an experience of unconditional love and the call to parenthood as the highest of our callings.

For Luther, marriage and parenthood was the norm; today we live with many more configurations of home. Although Sara and I fit the traditional configuration of being married with a child, many of our friends do not. There are many ways for people today to develop a sense of home. I can speak only out of my experience as married to Sara and father to Douglas.

We were married the same year I entered Luther Seminary, in retrospect a great way to start a marriage. We were immediately invited into a marriage growth group with other married seminarians, learning how to fight fairly, to confront one another in love, and to face our shortcomings. This learning took place with great support from others of the same age and circumstance. Sara and I reflect back on how fortunate we were to have a community of friends who helped us begin our life together with loving accountability; this speeded up our development of a marriage that could embrace differences and conflict without going underground with our feelings and needs. We learned to express our needs and negotiate agreement on how they would be met. This took a lot of work, but it really paid off for both of us.

For Sara and me, our calling in the home has been a journey. The way I relate to Sara today is very different from the honeymoon love that ushered in our marriage. We both have different needs today and have many more subtle ways to express our care, understanding, and needs than when we were first married.

I spent the first years following my graduation from Luther Seminary in youth ministry. Sara was busy developing her career as a teacher. We decided to delay starting a family because we were both young idealists that thought we could be part of the 1960s promise that we could change the world, making it a better place.

When we finally did decide to have children, and after much testing, we faced the reality that our only option was to adopt. Little did we know that the process would end up taking several years. By the time Douglas John entered our lives, we had been married thirteen years.

When I became a parent, suddenly my way of talking about parenthood changed. I was far less forthcoming with suggestions on how to parent. Instead I found myself listening more to parents, seeking to develop parenting skills that would help me in what proved to be the biggest challenge of my life. We really enjoyed Douglas in those early years, but were also typically filled with all kinds of surprises, as any parent knows.

One of the surprises came on a Sunday afternoon when Douglas and I were out cross-country skiing. Douglas was six. At one point we stopped to rest. I showed Douglas how to make an angel in the snow by lying on my back and moving my arms and legs up and down in the snow. We had made several angels when I glanced at Douglas, who appeared to be crying without making a sound. I raced to his side, thinking that he had gotten frostbite. But as I picked him up and took him in, I realized something else was going on. When I asked him what was wrong, he said in words barely audible through his deep silent tears, "Daddy, you will never know the emptiness in my heart."

I remember feeling so confused and helpless. Not every child experiences this kind of profound abandonment at the age of six, but Douglas did. That event began five years of dealing with outbursts of tears at the most unexpected moments. As a father I really wanted to take this pain away from Douglas, to fix him. But I had no answers. All I could do was to hold him close to me as we shared the mystery of his feelings of abandonment.

One of the most dramatic of Douglas's outbursts came while we were at a restaurant on vacation. I don't know why, but on this occasion I started to cry right along with him and literally could not stop. My tears were out of frustration at these repeated episodes and my inability to alleviate the pain of the son I so dearly loved. I felt a failure in my calling as a father.

Finally on a retreat later that summer, I received clarity and insight into what it means to be a father. At the start of the retreat the leader asked that we share with at least one other what we left behind to come on this retreat. My thoughts immediately went to Douglas and my feelings of failure.

As I shared this with a friend, he did not give me advice, but simply asked, "When your son cries, do you hold him?"

"Yes, that's all I know to do."

"That's enough," he said. "All my life I've wished that my father would have held me just one time!"

At that moment I realized that my calling as a father was to faithfully be there with my son, not needing to be ready with clever answers or to fix Douglas but simply to be present with him in the moment, as my father had done so many times with me.

In our callings at home we are given the opportunity to provide the encouragement so necessary for our children to begin their awareness of God's loving claim on their lives as people who are not only unconditionally accepted but also capable of loving and serving others.

Called in Community

We are also called to serve in our communities—at the local level of township or county, small town or city, at the state and national level, and in all of God's world. Throughout history Christians have responded to the needs of the sick, dependent children, the elderly, the poor and hungry, the victims of injustice.

The needs are all around us. All we have to do is pick up a newspaper or listen to the radio or watch TV or log on to the Internet. In fact, a danger is that we can be so overwhelmed by the number of problems and the extent of the need that we are paralyzed into inaction.

What is an answer to such "compassion fatigue"?

One is to choose one need that we see as most urgent or compelling, one that most deeply arouses our compassion. We can't do it all. But we can make a difference in one problem area, whether it is world hunger, homelessness, peace, the needs of the elderly, whatever touches our heart. I have a plaque in my office that reads "Let my heart be broken by the things that break the heart of God." There are many situations that break the heart of God. We can't feel them all or do something about them all, but we can do something.

Find something you can do that elicits your deep gladness, that gives you joy and satisfaction. This is not selfishness, this is realism. If you try to do work for which you are not gifted, if you try to help in ways that do not give you joy, you will not stay at it for long. You will soon burn out. For example, if you are an introvert, you will probably be worn out by an endless round of committee meetings. On the other hand, if you are an extrovert, you will want to do something with other people, because you get energy from that kind of interaction, while the introvert might gain energy by doing research, writing a report, keeping financial records, stuffing envelopes. Look for one thing to do that you believe in and find a way to make a difference with joy. Look toward your trusted friends and fellow believers to help you discern your call to action.

Another resource that can prevent you from being overwhelmed by all the world's problems is your membership in a community like a congregation or a service organization. Being in a community means I don't have to do and be everything. There are others with their unique calls and their unique concerns who can do what I cannot. I am set free to play my role in ways that are appropriate to my gifts and helpful to others.

Called in Congregation

Another domain for our calling is the church, especially the local congregation, but also other expressions of church, such as a synod or denomination or interdenominational Christian organizations. We will discuss the role of the congregation in further detail in chapter 5, but here we will explore the congregation as a place of service. The local congregation offers calls to two kinds of service. One is the call to assist in the internal functions of the congregation—assisting with teaching, finances, maintenance, the care of people within the congregation. A second form is when a congregation is the channel to service in the community, as when members operate a food pantry or volunteer at a soup kitchen or work on a Habitat for Humanity project.

A Dynamic, Ever-Renewed Call

The calling of God is a process, not a fixed system. We are not called to a job, for example, and then required to stay in it the rest of our lives. In fact, God may call us out of one work into another in God's own time. At times we are like Abraham, being called out of a familiar place to one we do not know. God's call enkindles our faith.

God's call is sometimes discerned through the closing of doors. In the closing of doors, the constraints of our life, we may find that singleness of heart for which we're created, the birthright gift that's in us. Early in life most of us appreciate having many options open to us, but at some point, if we want to make a difference in the world, we need to make some commitments to specific courses of action.

Not each chapter of our life is the same. Certain chapters provide limitations as well as new opportunities. For example, if we are parents of small children, we may choose to give them the majority of our attention and may not be as free to do community or political work. On the other hand, in retirement years, when we no longer have to pursue a job full time for a salary, we may have more time to devote to volunteer work.

Discerning God's call is an ongoing process. Even with the best of intentions we don't always get it right. We are fallible and sinful human beings, affected by our own past and the culture around us.

There is a difference between call and seduction. We are seduced at times by our own wishful thinking, by trying to live out someone else's call, by trying to imitate another person with different gifts from our own, or by trying to live out other people's vision for us. The Bible promises that "the truth will make you free" (John 8:32). The truth about God, God's will for the world, and the truth about myself sets me free from false callers, false expectations, false strengths.

Such seductions are not the call of God. In the ongoing process of discernment, we can correct our course. God forgives us when we misread the signals and frees us to make better choices.

Amid all our calls to serve in workplace, home, community, and congregation we need to keep in perspective our service with the stewardship of our own physical, mental, and spiritual health. This is part of our process of discernment. There are times when we can't do it all or have it all. We need to step back, take a sabbatical, seek help, let someone else take over.

In *Cry Pain, Cry Hope,* Elizabeth O'Connor wrote:

> Every single one of us has a "good work" to do in life. The good work not only accomplishes something needed in the world, but completes something in us. When it is finished, a new work emerges that will help us make green a desert place, as well as to scale another mountain in ourselves. The work we do in the world, when it is true vocation, always corresponds in some mysterious way to the work that goes on within us.[10]

Discerning God's Call

Some people think of call as very dramatic, as with the apostle Paul, being knocked off his horse, blinded, seeing a vision of Christ in heaven (Acts 9). But most often God uses ordinary natural means. How then do we recognize God's call?

1. By discerning our gifts

The Bible teaches us that God gives gifts to everyone, gifts differing from one person to another. Paul wrote to the Christians in Corinth: "Now there are varieties of gifts, but the same Spirit; and there are varieties of services, but the same Lord; and there are varieties of activities, but it is the same God who activates all of them in everyone. To each is given the manifestation of the spirit for the common good" (1 Corinthians 12:4-7).

These gifts that God has given us are a major clue as to the ways in which each of us can make a difference in the world. Sally Peters of Centered Life Initiative says:

> There is freedom in knowing what we were created to be. We find meaning and purpose in our lives when we understand that we were created by God with unique gifts and strengths, to serve God by serving and loving our neighbors. Knowing my strengths leads me to an understanding of what God has called me to be. Sometimes, even more importantly, it helps me know what I was not created to be.

Sometimes others are better able to identify our gifts than we ourselves. This is another reason to be in a "holding community" where others can help us to rightly discern our gifts. In chapter 4 we will explore further the opportunity and challenge of using our specific gifts to continue God's work of creation.

2. Looking at our context

Luther taught people that to discover their callings they need to look at their circumstances, the context of their life. The calling of God is probably not in some faraway place, but right in front of you. Consider your roles as spouse, parent, employee or employer, colleague, citizen, friend, member of the community. Be open to the needs you see around you—and beyond that in larger society, and you will begin to see where God is calling you to act right now in the place where you are.

3. Prayer

I believe that if we ask God, "Lord, what do you want me to do?" God will show us. So a first and ongoing step is to pray every day that you may discern the call of God and act accordingly.

4. Listening to your life

My friend and Quaker educator Parker Palmer has written a small book titled *Let Your Life Speak: Listening for the Voice of Vocation*. In it he suggests many helpful ways in which we can look inward to reflect on our own life experience, listening for the inner voice that reveals our various callings. Palmer says:

> Vocation does not come from willfulness. It comes from listening. I must listen to my life and try to understand what it is truly about—quite apart from what I would like it to be about—or my life will never represent anything real in the world, not matter how earnest my intentions.
>
> That insight is hidden in the word *vocation* itself, which is rooted in the Latin for "voice." Vocation does not mean a goal that I pursue. It means a calling that I hear. Before I can tell my life what I want to do with it, I must listen to my life telling me who I am. I must listen for the truths and values of the heart of my own identity, not the standards by which I must live—but the standards by which I cannot help but live if I am living my own life.[11]

5. Blessed in Community

In the 1800s the Scottish poet Robert Burns wrote: "O would some power the giftie give us, to see ourselves as others see us." As we've already noted, it may be others who can help us recognize the gifts we have or to let us know when we are trying to operate with gifts we do not have. The perceptions of others can help us discern the difference between seduction and a true call.

6. Joy

When we are operating from our gifts, we usually experience joy and energy because we are doing that for which we are made. My spiritual director, Bill Smith, said to me, "You know when there's a calling in your life, Jack. It's when it happens naturally to you, when it seems just like it's the easiest thing in the world, you do it easily, and you're meeting some obvious need—a need obvious to you though it may not be to others. When you're in the center of God's power in your life, you are naturally 'in the groove.' You feel completely fulfilled with a deep sense of optimism and hope, even as you address some of life's most difficult problems."

What you are called to do in a particular situation may be difficult. In fact, it will be if you are taking your deep gladness into a situation of deep need. But if you persevere, there will also be moments of joy and self-fulfillment and empowerment by the Spirit of God.

In their helpful book *Healing the Purpose of Your Life,* Dennis Linn, Sheila Fabricant Linn, and Matthew Linn talk about finding one's life purpose as discovering one's "sealed orders."

> Because our sealed orders are our connection to our own life force, following them not only helps us overcome fears and obstacles, but also protects us from burnout. Burnout comes not from doing too many things, but from doing things that are not meaningful

to us. However, those "doings" that we do find mean-ingful evoke the boundless energy of the life force within us. Put another way, our sealed orders come from God, and when we follow them we tap into the creative power of God. It is then that the same Spirit—the same power—that raised Jesus from the dead is at work within us. (Rom. 8:11)[12]

Four Qualities of a Call

Years ago Mary Crosby, cofounder of the Church of Our Savior in Washington, D.C., reported on the results of her study of God's callings in the Old Testament. She con-cluded that there were four qualities of a call, and these still apply to a call today.

1. A call tends to be simple and direct.

This does not always seem to be true when you are in a confusing or distressful circumstance, and it does not mean that you always know the specifics of what you have to do or are settled on whether you want to do it—or can. For example, it probably is a clear and direct call for you to take care of your aged father. But a decision about whether it's time for dad to go into a nursing home is still difficult. Yet the call itself is clear and direct.

In my experience, what I am called to do is usually not that mysterious. It's not like some one secret that God hides, and I have to try to find it out or suffer God's anger. What I am called to do is made clear to me, day by day, in my ordinary life. Sometimes it is only in hindsight that we see the simplicity that is on the other side of complexity.

2. A call is impossible for us to achieve on our own.

This does not mean that it is some bizarre circumstance requiring extraordinary powers. Just ask any parent. Being a good parent, especially in today's culture, is something we can't do by ourselves. We need the power of God and the support of others.

3. A call is usually a "minority movement," often countercultural, going against the grain of our society and its values.

You may seek support counsel from others, but ultimately, it has to be your own response to God's call. I remember going to my father and saying, "Dad, I can't decide whether to get married to Sara or not. Can you tell me what to do?" he said, "Well, personally, I love Sara a lot, but you are the one who will be living with her, so it has to be your decision."

4. The call happens in community.

Normally the call comes to us in the community of the family, the neighborhood, the workplace, the city or country in which we live. The community supplies not only the call but the means and support we need to fulfill that call.

Gregory S. Clapper points to the true value of a Christian's call in all of life:

> Leading a life of Christian vocation will almost certainly not always be what you thought it would be, and at times it probably will not be what you want it to be. It will, though, be the life that satisfies your deepest heartfelt longing. It will be the life worth living.[13]

The call of God on our lives is good news, but it is also threatening, awesome news. How can we carry out what God is calling us to do in the home, workplace, community, and congregation? The answer is that with the call God also sets us free from whatever binds us, liberating us to use our unique gifts to make God's world a better place. We turn to that subject in chapter 4.

Questions for Reflection and Discussion

1. Have you ever thought of yourself as "a little Christ"? How do you respond to the phrase?

2. How do you understand the relationship between grace and vocation?

3. What does "work" mean to you? How is your work a calling from God? In what ways does your work bless and serve others?

4. What is "home" and "family" for you? In what ways are you called in your home?

5. How are you actively serving in the public arena—local community, politics, volunteer organizations, the larger world?

6. How are you presently serving in your congregation? Are there other calls there for you? Are there activities you should let go of?

7. Have you ever experienced God's leading through the closing of doors?

8. How do you balance your various callings with the need to be a good steward of your own life?

9. How can you distinguish between a seduction and a call?

10. How does each of these help you discern your various calls?
    Your gifts
    The context of your life
    Prayer
    Listening to your life
    Community
    Joy

11. What was most helpful or interesting to you in this chapter?

Chapter 4

Set Free to Work with God

In my second year of college I was pursuing a pre-med degree with the goal of becoming a surgeon. But in my chemistry class, I realized that I was more interested in the people in my class than I was in science. I also met Sara, who in time became my wife. In those throes of first love, Sara and I got together every day—twenty-eight days in a row—for pizza. Needless to say, we were not so much interested in the menu!

The result was that my grade point average that quarter plummeted to 1.59. In those days grades were still sent to parents, so it was not surprising that one day I received a call from my father. "Hello, son, I just received your grades. It sounds as if you have a real challenge ahead, especially with the draft waiting to send you to Vietnam. What is of equal concern is that I looked at your cancelled checks, and I notice that you wrote twenty-eight checks to a pizza parlor. Now I know that no son of mine would buy pizza for twenty-eight straight days, especially when I have already paid for his room and board, so I assume you are buying stock in this pizza restaurant. But let's not talk about it on the phone. I think it would be better if your mom and I drove down to see you on Saturday. Goodbye."

I received Dad's call on Wednesday and I spent the next days in fear and trembling. On Saturday morning I waited by the door of my frat house so I could intercept Dad in the parking lot rather than be embarrassed by the encounter in front of other people.

As I walked to the car, Dad was just getting out. I was looking down out of shame and embarrassment at my failure and lack of judgment.

"Son, look at me!" he said. "I've taught you to look at me when I'm talking to you."

"I can't, Dad, because . . . well, I don't have any stock in the pizza parlor . . . and I've fallen in love . . . and I'm not sure what that means, because I've never been there before. I spent the money buying pizza and dating Sara. I've lost interest in becoming a doctor, but I'm not sure what it is I want to do. I know I have let you and Mom down." As I approached him, I wasn't sure what he would do.

To my incredible surprise and relief, he put his hands on my shoulders and said, "Mom and I drove three hundred miles to let you know how much we love you. We love you as much when you goof up as when you excel. Sometimes it's easier to understand love at a time of failure. We're confident in you and your abilities. You have it within you to figure out your future. You can do it, and we are proud of you, and we stand with you."

With that, he got in the car and began the six-hour drive back home.

His forgiveness and acceptance set me free from the burden of my shame and guilt at letting him down; it did not set me free from responsibility. I knew I was still expected to live up to my family's standards, but Dad's word of grace set me free and made me determined to figure out my plans for the future.

Freedom from Bondage

In one of the most dramatic encounters in the Gospels, Jesus met a man we would call unemployed, a man possessed by "an unclean spirit," who lived among the tombs (Mark 5:1-20). The man was in a bad way: "No one could restrain him any more even with a chain; for he had often been restrained with shackles and chains, but the chains he wrenched apart, and the shackles he broke in pieces; and no one had the strength to subdue him. Night and day among the tombs and on the mountains he was always howling and bruising himself with stones" (vv. 3-5). When this unfortunate man saw Jesus, he called out for help. Jesus cast the unclean spirits out of the man and into a herd of swine—unclean animals for the Jews.

The neighboring people were so amazed to see the man now "clothed and in his right mind" (v. 15) that their only response was to ask Jesus to leave. The healed man begged Jesus that he might go with him, to join the twelve disciples as one of his followers. Jesus refused his offer and said, "Go home to your friends, and tell them how much the Lord has done for you, and what mercy he has shown you" (v. 19).

Here was a man set free by Jesus and then called not to a different life, but to stay in his present situation and be a witness to his friends and neighbors of God's saving action.

In the Lutheran liturgy we confess: "We are in bondage to sin and cannot free ourselves."[1] In this understanding, sin is not limited to immoral deeds we do, but describes the conditions in which we live, the system in which we are trapped. We may be in bondage to the expectations of others, the structures of our society that keep us from developing our gifts, our inordinate need to compare ourselves with others, our dependence on the approval of others. From all these we are being freed by God's word of forgiveness and by the power of the Holy Spirit. We confess that we cannot free ourselves from this bondage, but are dependent on God and on the Christian community, on those who love us.

In *The Meaning of Success,* Michel Quoist wrote in a chapter "How to Be Free":

> By becoming obedient even to death, Jesus Christ has won genuine freedom for you. By dying with him to sin, you will free yourself from every form of slavery and will rise with him to a new life of freedom. . . . You will be fully free when you have wedded yourself without reserve, once and for all, to your Liberator.[2]

Set Free from What?

The grace of God sets us free from the need to earn our own salvation, from having to prove our self-worth by what we do, by our accomplishments. Our self-worth is already guaranteed by God, sealed in our baptism. Liberated from the need to justify ourselves or earn our standing with God, we are free to serve our neighbor, the people around us, even people in far places.

We are set free from the game of "compare and contrast." We no longer need to compare ourselves with others and to have more than they have or accomplish more than they do. Instead you can look to God as your Center and at the way God has created you with your unique set of gifts and abilities and passions. Others no longer have to lose in order for you to feel good about yourself.

Related to this, a life centered in God frees us from consumerism and drive for money and success. One woman described how her daughter was set free from a search for status and money when someone who knew her well helped her recognize her dependable strengths of nurturing and teaching young children and encouraged her toward a vocation as an elementary school teacher.

With a life centered in God, you are set free from a sense of meaninglessness. Knowing that God your Center has given you gifts, called you, and sent you to serve in God's world, you have a reason for living. There are ways in which you can make a difference. This is true even for those who are elderly or limited in mobility.

We are set free from self-absorption for self-giving. Your needy self is no longer the center of your life. With God as your Center, you are able to think not in terms of "what's in it for me?" but instead in terms of "what do I have to give the neighbor?" This does not mean that we should never care for ourselves. We are called to be good stewards also of our own mental and physical and spiritual health. Self-care then is not just for self-gratification but also to allow us to be more self-giving. We will look more in chapter 5 at how you can find the nurture and support you need for a centered life.

We are set free from the feeling of hopelessness, that there is nothing we can do that makes a difference. God can take whatever you have to offer and make something of it—like the boy who brought a few fish and a few loaves to Jesus, who used it to feed more than five thousand people (John 6:1-14).

We are set free from the fear of failure or the need to be right. Assured of God's grace and forgiveness by God's word of promise, we can dare to move, to risk, to falter, and to fail. Every day gives us a new opportunity to live out the meaning of our baptism, in a daily dying and rising again.

Sally Peters, manager of the Centered Life Initiative, says: "Another kind of freedom comes when I give up perfectionism and the need to control and instead focus on daily faithfulness. When I consider that success or failure is not ultimately in my hands but God's, I am free to act faithfully, to do the best I can with the strengths I have, and not worry so much about the outcome."

We are set free from paralyzing fear—fear of our own safety or success. After Jesus' capture and death, his disciples were huddled in fear (John 20:19-23). Jesus came among them and the first thing he said was, "Peace be with you." He set them free from fear to live in his peace. The next thing he said was, "As the Father has sent me, so I send you." Jesus was sending them right back out into the world that had crucified him. For them this would have been an impossible calling if Jesus had not also said, "Receive the Holy Spirit." As God the Father had sent Jesus, Jesus was now sending them, with the power and guidance of the Holy Spirit.

A setting-free moment for me happened one day when I was six or seven, walking with my dad on Seventh Street in Rockford, Illinois, on that part of the street lined with bars. As good Methodists, my family did not drink, dance, or smoke. Those were important values for us; they helped define who we were. My dad and I bought something in a hardware store, then started walking down the street past all the bars. I started doing what I thought would win favor with my dad; I badmouthed the drunks and the stinky taverns, asking whether we could walk on the other side of the street. Just then a drunk came staggering out of one bar, bumped into my dad, then into a parking meter, and fell to the ground.

My dad went to the man and said, "Sir, can I help you up? Are you all right?"

The man, in his inebriated state, tried to put his arms around my dad to hug him, and expressed his maudlin thanks. Dad gently lowered the man's arms and steadied him.

As we moved on down the street, I looked up at my dad in surprise. Continuing to walk, he said, "That man was a little boy once who had dreams like you."

I believe that God acted in that moment to set me free from my stereotypes and judgmentalism. My dad still held to his own personal rules, but he transcended his own standards for the sake of this person. And I was set free to see this stranger in a new way.

On the first Easter weekend, two followers of Jesus were walking to a village called Emmaus (Luke 24:13-35). Filled with confusion and sorrow and hopelessness, they were discussing the disturbing events of Jesus' capture, torture, and death. Suddenly along the road a stranger joined their sorrowful walk. He asked them, "What are you discussing with each other while you walk along?" They said,

> Are you the only stranger in Jerusalem who does not know the things that have taken place here in these days? . . . The things about Jesus of Nazarath, who was a prophet almighty in deed and word before God and all the people. . . . But we had hoped that he was the one to redeem Israel. . . . Moreover, some women of our group astounded us. They were at the tomb early this morning, and when they did not find his body there,

they came back and told us that they had indeed seen a vision of angels who said that he was alive.

They had thought to inform this stranger about Jesus, but the stranger, Jesus himself, opened their understanding of the Messiah, that God's chosen one would not come as a military conqueror to shock and awe the Romans, but as a suffering servant.

When they approached the village, the disciples seemed to be so fascinated by this stranger's teaching that they invited him into their lives. And there, as they sat around a table and Jesus broke the bread, their eyes were opened. They were awakened to his true identity.

As suddenly as he appeared, Jesus was gone. The disciples looked at one another and said, "Were not our hearts burning within us while he was talking to us on the road, while he was opening the scriptures to us?" (Luke 24:32). Through the words of scripture and the fellowship of the table this stranger had set these disciples free from their sorrow, their hopelessness, their misunderstanding of the Messiah.

It is important to recognize that God's work of setting us free is not yet finished. The signs of suffering and bondage are all around us. The Bible pictures the earth as still in bondage, groaning as it awaits the final liberation (Romans 8:18-23). We live in the hope that in the fullness of time, the whole creation will be set free from suffering and death. In the meantime we live with God's promise: "We know that all things work together for good for those who love God, who are called according to his purpose" (Romans 8:28).

Set Free for What?

In *Our Lives Are Not Our Own,* Rochelle Melander and Harold Eppley write:

> God's saving act in Jesus does more than free us from the bondage of sin. God's act frees us *for* service to God, the community of faith, and the world. In loving gratitude to God for all that God has done for us, we live accountable both to God and to one another.
>
> In a sense, because we no longer have to worry about our status in the realm of God—we are free to act boldly *for* the welfare of others. The "pressure" is off. The outcome has been decided. We don't have to worry that our actions or missteps will somehow lose us the keys to the kingdom. What we do with our lives says "thank you" to God; it's our gift back to God for all that God has done for us. We have been made free by God, and in that gracious state, we can use all that God has given us to act on behalf of others and the world. We are free to be the words and hands of Jesus to those we meet each day.[3]

I think of my friend Doug, who had been the owner and manager of a large construction and real-estate corporation that carried out major building projects, including government-sponsored affordable housing. The business was very prosperous, although a great deal of money was tied up in projects that would not break even for a few years. Then in 1986 the federal government changed the tax code in ways that cost companies like Doug's millions of dollars. Suddenly Doug's company was in deep trouble.

He recalls:

At this time I was almost paralyzed by the fear of failure, the fear of losing face, the fear of being broke for the first time in my life. I could have chosen to declare bankruptcy and let others suffer the consequences, but that didn't seem right to me. One morning in my time of Bible reading and prayer, trying to cope with my fear of failure and poverty, I glanced at a needlepoint piece a niece had made for me. It listed the gifts of the Holy Spirit in Galatians 5: love, joy, peace, patience, kindness, generosity, faithfulness, gentleness, and self-control. It was as if the Holy Spirit was saying directly to me, "Doug, all the things you really want in life—like love, joy, and peace—are free." And in that moment I was freed up from the fear of going broke, the fear of failure. I saw that even being poor and unsuccessful, I could have love, joy, and peace, and the other absolutely free gifts of the Spirit.

My goal then was to salvage as much as possible for the investors, our employees, and for myself. In order to do this, I had to sell the construction part of the business, which was very dear to me. I divided this up into several smaller companies that I sold to former employees, enabling them to begin their own ventures. I used that money to fund other projects. In that way I was able to pay all the suppliers and subcontractors. The last creditor left was the bank that had loaned me the initial capital. I made a "workout agreement" with the bank, and I worked nineteen years to pay back the principal and millions of dollars worth of interest. And now I am free and clear.

Doug moved on in his life to put more attention into new ways of creating affordable housing for people. He also found meaning in serving in his congregation, in growing spiritually, and in nourishing friendships. "The spiritual part of my life is energizing me more than ever before," he told me.

When God frees us, it is not just freedom for the sake of freedom. It is not escapism or freedom for self-indulgence. We are free to exercise our vocation in the world. We are free to follow Jesus as his disciples, drawn to him in love.

Drawn, Not Driven

Jesus declared, "No one can come to me unless drawn by the Father who sent me; and I will raise that person up on the last day" (John 6:44). He reinforced this when he said, "You did not choose me but I chose you" (John 15:16).

Being drawn by the love of God, not driven by our need to perform, is the result of a grace-filled life. One of my hardest lessons continues to be how to live out of the "blessedness" claimed for me at my baptism. My primary struggle has been finding my identity in *whose* I am and *who* I am, rather than from *what I do*. My contemporary society has tried to convince me to define myself externally, by comparing myself and competing with others according to how I look and how well I perform. In high school, I was driven to believe that if I was an A student, I was an A person; if I was a B student, I was a B person. If I was an F student, I was a total failure. I was driven by my needs to compete and achieve. I needed to learn to allow God to draw me in love.

Bill Smith, my friend and spiritual mentor, often reminded me: "Live out of your chosenness. Rest in the love of God." I am drawn, first and foremost, to the

Father through Jesus, by the power of the Holy Spirit. From this drawing I get my identity and my calling. Jesus promises to be with us, even to the point of lifting us up on the last day.

One person who was drawn to God through Jesus was Nicodemus, whose story we read in John 3. Nicodemus was a successful businessman and a leader of his religious community. I can imagine that when Nicodemus walked down the street, mothers pointed him out to their children and said, "When you grow up, you could be like Nicodemus." Yet despite his outer successes, Nicodemus was empty inside; he lacked a center.

He came to Jesus at night, searching for more than he knew. Jesus confronted him with the sharp words, "You must be born again." He was leading Nicodemus to the insight that he needed God's Spirit to come into his life and transform it. And in this dialogue Jesus taught one of the most treasured statements about God: "For God so loved the world that he gave his only Son, so that everyone who believes in him may not perish but may have eternal life" (John 3:16). Here is God's great "everyone": God's love and forgiveness and acceptance is for all the whosoevers in the world—even me! And in that "whosoever love" of God I find a dependable center for my life.

Being drawn frees me from being driven by guilt or by other people's expectations or my own need for achievement. I am set free to look at my own gifts and see how they can be used for God's purposes in the world.

An Active God

Theologian Darrell Jodock has said:

> For Luther, God is at work everywhere—in families, in the workplace, in the public life of the community, in international affairs—everywhere. This ubiquitous activity does not mean, of course, that God causes everything that happens—indeed, much of what happens does not at all please God and is contrary to God's purposes—but God is nonetheless at work, amid the ambiguity and the conflict, to enhance human dignity and to advance the cause of justice.[4]

In *Listen! God Is Calling!* D. Michael Bennuthum names some of the ways God is at work in the world:

> God cares about the world, so much so that God continues to be at work in it. God is at work in and through the lives of people, all people—whether they are aware of it or not, whether they are Christian or not. How exciting it can be for believers to discover this activity of God where they least expect it, in the everyday. How affirming it is for them to realize that they are, in effect, agents of God in the ongoing work of creation and even 'means of grace' as they function as the channels thought which others experience God's love.[5]

What is our basic stance as we seek to be "agents of God in the ongoing work of creation"? Are we arrogant in thinking we can be cocreators with God? In his famous essay "The Freedom of the Christian," Martin Luther wrote one of his most profound paradoxes: "A Christian is a perfectly free Lord of all, subject to none. A Christian is a perfectly dutiful servant of all, subject to all."[6] In being free to serve, the Christian is following Jesus, who came not to be served, but to serve, to suffer, to give his life to redeem all of God's creation to be "the man for others," as Dietrich Bonhoeffer named him. We are set free to serve in each of the four domains: workplace, home, community, and congregation, using our own unique pattern of gifts and values.

Finding Your Unique Gifts

In *How to Find Your Mission in the World*, Richard Bolles writes about finding what we can do to make the world a better place, through identifying our gifts and using the guidance of the Holy Spirit. Your unique mission on earth, according to Bolles, is:

a. to exercise that Talent which you particularly came to Earth to use

b. in those place(s) in setting(s) which God has caused to appeal to you the most,

c. and for those purposes which God most needs to have done in the world.[7]

Awareness of our gifts allows us to participate in the world in a way that is rich and fulfilling for us but also that contributes to the common good. Awareness of our gifts helps us make good choices in the use of our time and energy. Awareness of our gifts connects us with a sense of calling and mission.

Because of our own limitations and the possibilities of various forms of unconscious self-deception, discerning our strengths occurs best in a community, probably a small group, in which we are safe and supported by people who care for us.

Below is an exercise, developed by the Centered Life Initiative of Luther Seminary, that can help you discern your gifts. You can do it on your own, but it is even more beneficial if you use it also with a group.

Personal Exercise:
Discerning Your Dependable Strengths™
Think of a "good experience" from your own life—an event, activity, or time that meets *all three* of the following criteria: something you feel you did well, enjoyed doing, and are proud of having done.

What did you love to do when you were ten years old?

What activities give you the most pleasure when you are not at work? Give two or more examples.

Think of a recent activity or work experience. Which parts did you do best and enjoy most?

After leaving high school, which two or three subjects or topics did you study and enjoy most?

Group Exercise

In groups of four people:

Think of a "good experience" from your own life—an event, activity, or time that meets *all three* of the following criteria: something you feel you did well, enjoyed doing, and are proud of having done.

Share your good experience with the group. Listen to each person as they tell their "good experience."

Discuss possible strengths, talents, and abilities each person used in their good experience.

Living by Your Values

Pastor Chris Bellefeuille of St. Barnabas Lutheran Church in Plymouth, Minnesota, said this in a sermon:

God desires that we live lives in service to God, lives of discipleship. And we have each been uniquely gifted for that task. The problem is that we have limited our understanding of serving God to things that involve the words: committee, mission, evangelism, or church. And these are good and important things. But our service to God is not limited to the things that fall neatly into those categories. Everything, every moment of our lives can be service to God.

A centered life is a life where we live out the values that have been shaped and informed by our Christian faith in everything we do. . . . No one can tell you what exactly your faith-based values are or what they should be. That is why a centered life requires of each of us some time for self-examination and prayer.

If you think about every moment of your life as a moment of discipleship, it can be a bit overwhelming. But every moment of your life is an opportunity for discipleship. God has given each of us many great gifts: like time, money, material things, relationships, and our particular talents. As Christian people, we use all of these gifts to live out our values in the world. Think of discipleship as minute-by-minute stewardship of these gifts: how are they being spent, to what purpose are they being directed? We are constantly making choices about how we use those gifts. Whether it feels like it or not, everything we do in our day is a choice.[8]

Personal Exercise: Exploring Your Values

Identify five of your top values drawn from your deep convictions of faith (for example, family, kindness, service, devotion to God). Write them down.

Now make a list of all the ways you spend your time. Make a list of the daily things: eating, bathing, reading the paper. Then make a list of weekly things like laundry, worship, taking out the trash.

Now look at your list. If someone else were to read your list, what would it tell them about your values?

What does it tell you? How well does it reflect the five values you identified?

If it does not reflect your values well, what changes in your life might you want to make?

Bellefeuille continues:

> What I like about this way of thinking about your life is that each of our values are subtly different and the way we use our time, money, talents, and care for our relationships will look different for each of us. But each minute of every day is a discipleship minute, even the moments spent on fun and relaxation. We feel more centered, less anxious, more integrated when what we do reflects more closely what we really value. And those values are shaped and formed by the grace and forgiveness we have received from God.[9]

Set Free for a Lived Faith

Being set free to use and discern our gifts is a lifelong process. It is the most important and difficult process in our lives. On our own, we find it an overwhelming task. But the good news is that we are not meant to do it alone. We are made for community. In a safe and loving group we can find the nurture and support we need for a centered life. We turn to that essential topic in chapter 5.

Questions for Reflection and Discussion

1. Think back on my college story at the beginning of the chapter and on the story of Doug. How was each of us set free *from* and set free *for?* Can you identify a similar event in your own life?

2. Refer back to the section, "Set Free from What?" In which conditions or situations have you most

experienced bondage or unfreedom? In what ways have you been set free? Where do you still feel in need of freedom?

3. How do you understand the difference between being drawn and being driven?

4. How would you answer the question: What *in the world* is God doing?

5. What do you see as your dependable strengths? How might God use them to achieve divine purposes on earth?

6. What are the values by which you live? How does the way you spend your time and money match up with these values?

7. What did you find most interesting or helpful in this chapter?

Chapter 5

Finding Nurture and Support for Living Out Your Callings

I was talking to a businessman from Oregon who runs a very large corporation and asked him, "How are you doing, leading this whole organization? What role is the church playing with you?"

He said, "I'm an active member of my church, and my family is very involved, but I'm sorry to say that my church doesn't have much to say to me about how I run this organization. In fact, probably the last place I'd go is to the pastor, because I've listened to enough sermons to realize he has a bias toward someone like me, a producer of goods and services. Though I love this man and appreciate his life and what he's done for my family, he is not a resource for me when it comes to living my life out from Monday to Sunday."

"Well, don't you go to church?" I asked.

"I go to church every Sunday. In fact my pastor would probably say I'm a model member, and I give quite a lot to it. I have the yearning to find answers to the tough questions I face day in and day out, but I've had to look outside my congregation for that help."

"So where did you go?" I asked.

"Oh, there are many ways that people in my position gather together to try to figure that out."

"What if your congregation was a place that really did offer you resources and supported you and sent you into your world of work with the kind of validation offered to any other ministry of that congregation? What difference would that make to you?"

"I'd begin by giving a lot more money to a place that really had value for me. But I just can't believe that would ever happen. I think there are a lot of people out there in the business community who are yearning for that experience."

Although this successful businessman did find a valid and valuable source of support through friends, he still had the yearning for the church where he worshiped on Sunday to somehow relate more effectively to Monday. He puts into words the question being asked my many congregations, "How can we, as a congregation, be more effective in equipping and sending our members into the world of work?"

The Present and the Future

Lay people and pastors from six congregations worked together for five years to identify what is needed in congregations to help people connect Sunday with Monday to Saturday. The drawing below reflects how they viewed the congregation in its present state.[1]

- What do you see in this image?
- What does it mean to you?
- Can you identify with the tension that is portrayed?
- How realistically does this reflect your life?

The same group of people created the drawing below to illustrate their vision of how they would like to see the congregation's presence in the world.

Take a moment to reflect on this drawing.

- How do you interpret it?
- Is this a positive image for you?
- What are some things that block this from becoming a reality?

The drawing illustrates the church as God's people sent into all sorts of places to live out their callings. After the group drew this picture of their preferred future for the church, they realized that they had visualized Jesus' words in John 15:5: "I am the vine, you are the branches. Those who abide in me and I in them bear much fruit."

I believe that there is great potential for congregations to offer just the nurture and support that helps people live out their faith in their daily lives in the workplace, the family, and the community. I believe that congregations are the best places for God's people to be inspired and equipped to live out their callings each day. I envision congregations as places where people gather, are cared for, equipped and validated for their everyday mission and ministry and then set free to serve God in their many vocational settings. Our needs for a place to belong and to make a difference in the world can come together in the congregation.

What the Congregation Has to Offer
Worship
Basic to all its other offerings, the congregation is the primary place where Christian believers come together for worship, to hear the word of God, to receive the blessings of baptism and Holy Communion, to sing God's praises, to bring before God the needs of the people and the world.

These blessings come in all congregations, but I believe that congregations could do more in worship to bridge the Sunday-Monday split. The gospel is proclaimed when God's good news for each person is connected to their "earthly" callings in the workplace, home, and community. What if the congregation prayed for people while they are alive, healthy, and working, not just when they are dying, sick, or unemployed? What if a worship service celebrated with a new sixteen-year-old driver by blessing her in her new role and reminding her of the responsibility that comes with that new freedom? What if we commissioned the work of all students, teachers, and school workers at the beginning of the school year instead of just the congregation's Sunday school staff?

When pastors spend time in the community, homes, and workplaces of members of the congregation, they reflect a better understanding of the daily joys and challenges of all people in prayers, sermon, and liturgies.

Teaching

Through sermons, Bible classes, retreats, and workshops, the congregation (and other expressions of the church) can offer Christian perspectives (which are often counter to the commonly promoted teachings of our society) on work, marriage, child rearing, and community service.

Support and Accountability Groups

The role of the congregation is to provide support and accountability, primarily in small groups that will encourage the discovery of each person's strengths and affirm the value of each member's gifts and calling. What if every person in the congregation knew what they excelled at and were celebrated and valued for their work—both inside and outside the congregation? What if members could clearly see how their gifts were necessary to the health of the body of Christ and that each person's strengths were valued? What if the full power of the people of God was unleashed through knowledge of their unique gifts and abilities and a clear sense of God's call for their lives?

My vision is for the congregation to be a "holding environment," a safe place in which people can bring all aspects of themselves into unity, a place where they can share both the pain and the promise of their lives, of their several callings. This happens when we know one another well enough to trust each other, when we can share our disappointments and fears, our joys and our tough questions about the "gray areas" of our lives. This can happen best in small groups which allow for individual sharing.

Sally Peters, manager of the Centered Life Initiative, reports on one such group:

> I am a member of a Bible-study group that meets every Tuesday at 6:30 A.M. The group is made up of ten to twelve women. It was started about thirteen years ago by a female associate pastor. The pastor selected our studies, sometimes with input from the group, and led us through it each week. She began each meeting by taking prayer requests and then praying for each one.
>
> After several years, the pastor left our congregation to take another call, and another associate pastor would not arrive for several months. We had to figure out what to do with the group. We loved meeting each week for prayer and study. Many commented on how they had come to rely on the support of the group and noticed a positive difference in their lives.
>
> We decided to colead the group. Members took turns listening to prayer requests, praying aloud for the group, and leading the study. As much as we had appreciated the pastor who began and led the group, now each person was nurtured in faith as we muddled though the lessons together, brought experiences of our own into the discussion, and shared our doubts, fears, and joys in the community of faith. When the pastor had been present, we deferred to her theological training to answer our questions and let her love us with her skills in pastoral care. When she was no longer there, we learned to seek the wisdom of the whole group and learned to love and care for each other.

Challenge

Congregations have in many places been good at gathering people and comforting them in times crisis, such as illness and grief, but the preacher's job is to comfort the afflicted and to afflict the comfortable. This applies also to the lay members of the congregation: while we support our fellow members who are in pain and need, we can also challenge one another to live out our faith in the family, the workplace, the political and social arenas.

A School of Prayer

The congregation can serve as a school of prayer where members and spiritual seekers can learn the Christian disciplines of prayer, meditation, journaling, and sabbath time— all practices that support our individual lives and callings.

Opportunities for Service

Congregations can be places that help us understand our unique giftedness and channel our talents and energies into meaningful service. This may be in the congregation itself, but hopefully also in forms of outreach to those outside the congregation. The congregation too is called to move from self-absorption to self-giving.

In the article "A Small Church Redefines Its Mission," Richard H. Bliese describes how one small struggling congregation on Chicago's south side where he served as a part-time "worker priest" moved from figuring out how to survive into a posture of mission.[2] They adopted this mission statement: "We are sent as a community of disciples and apostles to share God's love."

Because he had only limited time to spend at the church, Bliese called on the members to become ministers themselves. They let him know that they were already overly busy, overly burdened. He concluded: "It became apparent that our own congregational renewal was increasingly being fueled by assisting our people to live out their callings in their homes, communities, and workplaces, instead of focusing on our immediate churchly need to keep our programs well run."[3]

The congregation began Sunday LIFT forums (Living in Faith Together) to discuss ministry in daily life and Wednesday community nights to encourage people to grow in their faith and witness.

Bliese describes how they developed the first of three ministries that were carried out mainly by lay people. "The first major emphasis was mission to seniors. As we studied our neighborhood, we began to notice the high percentage of seniors living in their own homes but still in need of assistance. So we began our Senior Outreach Ministry." Today we help seventy seniors with everything from rides to the doctor's office to telephone reassurance. Twenty-two members of the congregation were trained for this weekly ministry.

Bliese said that the congregation members learned that their call was to the neighborhood, not just to the church. Almost none of the seniors served were members of the congregation. They also found that having lay people carry out the service to the seniors was more rewarding than paying a pastor to do it.

The other two ministries to which the congregation was called were to become an inclusive multicultural community and to reach out to the unchurched.

Models and Mentors

In the church we can find models and mentors—people who have experience in various forms of service in the workplace, in the family, the community, and the congregation. In addition to those people directly present in our lives, we have the examples of Christians throughout history and around the globe who offer us both inspiration and direction.

What Can You Do?

What if your congregation does not now offer the kind of support and nurture you feel you need to sustain your callings at work, in your family, in the community? Here are several suggestions.

First of all, before you criticize or seek to change things, be sure to participate in and support the efforts that are already taking place.

Second, ask for what you need. Ask your pastor or Christian education director to address these issues in sermons, to offer classes and workshops and retreats on these topics. Consider volunteering to help organize such efforts.

Third, begin a small group of like-minded individuals. Two or three gathered together in Jesus' name have the promise of his presence with them. Begin a support group for people dealing with work issues or family problems or community and world concerns.

Fourth, look beyond the congregation. Although the congregation is "home base" for church members, it is not the only expression of the church. The Evangelical Lutheran Church in America synods and the national churchwide offices offer resources and programs. Various parachurch organizations offer print and media resources, workshops, and ongoing programs.

Finally, rather than dropping out of the church altogether out of frustration, consider looking for another congregation that offers the nurture you need. You may be criticized for "church shopping," but don't let that stop you from getting the support you need.

Although much has been made in this book about the benefits of community, there are things we can do for ourselves, and this may be especially true for introverts.

Look anew at the long tradition of Christian spiritual disciplines or practices.

Practices That Support Your Calling

At best we spend an hour or two a week in worship or study or mutual support in a congregational setting. We can't expect that to meet all our needs in the other 160-some hours of the week. There is also the need for spiritual self-care through spiritual practices or disciplines of the Christian life. These practices can be learned in the congregation, at retreat houses or conferences, or through books, videotapes, and audiotapes. Two books from a Lutheran perspective can be highly recommended: *Practicing the Faith* (Dorothy Bass, ed.) and *The World According to God* (Martha Storz, see Recommended Reading). Martha Storz identifies the value of spiritual practices:

> Religious practices describe a relationship to the sacred. As a religion, Christianity is not primarily about assenting to doctrine or obeying a code, though these certainly figure. Christianity is primarily about being in relationship with the God revealed in Christ. The life of discipleship flows out of this relationship with the crucified and risen Christ.[4]

Congregations help people intentionally in God's presence beyond Sunday morning by encouraging them to practice their faith in everyday life through prayer, spiritual reading, journaling, and sabbath time. We were created with an inner hunger and need for God. The congregation can support members in leading centered lives by identifying and teaching practices that help members in their spiritual disciplines and reflect on their faith daily.

Prayer
I begin each morning with prayer and couldn't get through the day without it. Every morning I pray a prayer I learned from theology professor Charles Whiston. I imagine Christ standing at the foot of my bed saying to me:

> I am your Lord Jesus Christ:
> I was the agent of my Father in creating you;
> I died upon the cross for you.
> Therefore, you do not belong to yourself;
> you belong to me.
> Will you give yourself to me this day?

Then I pray my response:

> O Lord Jesus Christ:
> In obedience to your holy claim upon me,
> I give myself anew to you this day;
> all that I am,
> all that I have;
> to be wholly and unconditionally yours
> for your using.
> Take me away from myself, and
> use me up as you will,
> when you will, where you will,
> with whom you will.[5]

Such a prayer of dedication leads naturally to the practice of petition and intercession, as I bring my own needs and the needs of those of my family, my work, my community, and my congregation before God. All Christians are called to the life of prayer.

Marc Kolden mentions some ways in which prayer affects our various callings in daily life:

> Prayer reminds us that God cares about who are and also cares about our neighbors and what we do in our roles. Prayer gives us a true perspective on what otherwise often might seem to be just a bunch of trivial matters. Prayer opens us up to think about God's will for that situation, for those neighbors, and for the larger context. Through prayer God may give us new ideas, may open us to receive help from others whom we had ignored, or may help us to realize when there is nothing more we can do. Prayer should help us to say, "Not my will but thine be done, O Lord." It may lead us to acknowledge our sin and repent. In all of these ways, prayer offers ways for God to become part of the situation that had not been available before—at least not available through us and through and for those whom God has given us.[6]

Spiritual Reading

A second morning discipline for me is spiritual reading. I read the Bible or some other spiritual book and use this as a springboard for reflection and prayer. I record insights from my reading in my journal. The books listed in Recommended Reading, all dealing with different aspects of the centered life, would be appropriate for slow, reflective spiritual reading.

Journaling

A spiritual journal can be a valuable tool for the centered life, a place where all the varied aspects of your life can come together in the presence of God. I like this definition of a journal:

> A journal is a book in which you keep a personal record of events in your life, of your different relationships, of your response to things, of your feelings about things—of your search to find out who you are and what the meaning of your life might be. It is a book in which you carry out the greatest of life's adventures—the discovery of yourself.[7]

For years I've used a 5 x 7-inch spiral-bound notebook as a journal. Starting from the front of the notebook I write reflections on the Bible readings for the day as found in *The Book of Common Prayer*. Starting from the back of the book I write my ideas and thoughts about my life and work.

There are many ways that journal keeping can benefit you. For a sampling of some of them see Ron Klug, *How to Keep a Spiritual Journal*.

Sabbath Time

Still another spiritual practice from the Judeo-Christian tradition is that of sabbath, of times of rest in what for many is a hectic, overburdened schedule. Lutheran Bishop Mark Hanson describes his own need for sabbath:

> People are also reclaiming sabbath, or a rhythm of life that includes rest and renewal and refreshment. If my days don't have this ebb and flow, I end up being less than human. I need to include time for what is really

re-creative for me, like time in nature, time for music and reading.

Each person has to discover for himself or herself how to build in some time for solitude, reflection, simply being in the presence of God. If, like many people, we have busy, overloaded lives, the sabbath time may help us discern what God is calling us to do and be and of what we need to let go."[8]

You will need to discover your own spiritual practices and the times of day that works best for you.

Solitude and Community

The German Lutheran theologian Dietrich Bonhoeffer asserted that we need both solitude and community in our lives:

Only as we stand within the community can we be alone, and only those who are alone can be in community. Only in the community do we learn to be properly alone; and only in being alone do we learn to live properly in the community. It is not as if the one preceded the other; rather both begin at the same time, namely, with the call of Jesus Christ.[9]

While I carry out personal spiritual practices, I also depend on spiritual friends. A spiritual friend can be a pastor, parent, brother or sister, or friend. It has to be someone who loves you, who shares your faith, and is interested in being there for you and your calling. Bill and Anita Smith led a couples growth group while Sara and I attended Luther Seminary. They have walked with us and prayed for us for more than thirty years. I could always call Bill anytime, wherever I was in the world. What an amazing gift they have been to Sara and me in helping us remain faithful to our callings!

Another was Elizabeth Rooney until her death a few years ago. Filled with down-to-earth wisdom, she unveiled her insights through her wonderful gift of poetry. I would sit on her front porch and eat strawberries, and we would talk and pray together. It was important for me to have a female perspective; Elizabeth helped me see the world through a feminine lens.

I also have a group I call my personal board of directors. These are people, some living near me and some at a distance, to whom I look for support, counsel, and accountability. Who are the group of people who sustain you and nurture you in your various callings in the workplace, in the home, in the community, in the congregation?

At times when we are puzzled over our calling or needing to make a hard decision, we can gather a small group like this to help us come to clarity. The Quakers have a tradition of a "clearness committee" that is well worth emulating. In this process, the friends you have gathered listen as you state your dilemma. Then one by one they ask you questions to help you see more clearly. According to this method they are not allowed to give advice or recount their own experiences. They are simply to ask questions that help you come to your own insights into the situation.

Where Do We Go from Here?

Martin Luther wrote about the Christian life as an ongoing growth in holiness, as a process of becoming:

This life is not a being holy but a becoming holy; it is not a being well but a getting well; it is not a being but a becoming; it is not inactivity but practice.... As yet we are not what we ought to be, but we are getting there; the task is not yet accomplished and completed, but it is in progress and pursuit. The end has not yet been reached, but we are on the way that leads to it; as yet everything does not glow and sparkle, but everything is purifying itself.[10]

Our centered life is such a process of becoming. In this Spirit-led and Spirit-empowered movement, we look to God, who awakens us, calls us, frees us, and nurtures us.

A favorite prayer of mine touches on the basic themes of the centered life:

Lord God, you have called your servants
to ventures of which we cannot see the ending,
by paths as yet untrodden,
through perils unknown.
Give us faith to go out with good courage,
not knowing where we go,
but only that your hand is leading us
and your love supporting us;
through Jesus Christ our Lord.[11]

Questions for Reflection and Discussion

1. If you have not already done so, reflect on the two images of the congregation. In a group, share your responses.

2. What does your congregation presently offer you in your search for a centered life?

3. What else might the congregation offer that would be helpful to you?

4. What could you do to find the additional guidance and support you need?

5. Which spiritual practices do you engage in on a regular basis? Which might you add into your life?

6. Which people would you identify as spiritual friends? If you do not now have a spiritual friend, how might you find one?

7. Which people constitute your "personal board of directors"? Who sustains and nurtures you in your callings at work, in the home, in the community, in your congregation?

8. What are your next steps in seeking to live a centered life?

9. What did you find most interesting or helpful in this chapter?

Notes

Chapter 1. Longing for a Centered Life

1. Peter Vaill, *Learning As a Way of Being: Strategies for Survival in a World of Permanent Whitewater* (San Francisco: Jossey-Bass, 1996).
2. For helpful ways to handle information overload see Bob Sitze, *Not Trying Too Hard: New Basics for Sustainable Congregations* (Herndon, Va.: Alban Institute, 2001), 87-112.
3. Mark S. Hanson, *Faithful and Courageous: Christians in Unsettling Times* (Minneapolis: Augsburg Fortress, 2005), 11.
4. For further information on the Centered Life Initiative, write to Centered Life, Call 651-641-3444 or go online to www.centeredlife.org.
5. Chris Bellefeuille, www.centeredlife.org.
6. Edmund Steimle in *For All the Saints: A Prayerbook for and by the Church,* ed. Frederick J. Schumacher and Dorothy A. Zelenko (Delhi, N.Y.: American Lutheran Publicity Bureau, 1994), 447.
7. Evelyn Underhill, *The Spiritual Life* (London: Hodder & Stoughton, 1937), 36.

Chapter 2. Awakened to God's Presence

1. J. B. Phillips, Y*our God Is Too Small* (New York: Macmillan, 1961), 9.
2. Marc Kolden, *The Christian's Calling in the World* (St. Paul: Centered Life, 2002), 18.
3. Kolden, 23.
4. Rochelle Melander and Harold Eppley, *Our Lives Are Not Our Own: Saying "Yes" to God* (Minneapolis: Augsburg Fortress, 2003), 12-13.
5. Henri Nouwen, "A Spirituality of Waiting: Being Alert for God's Presence in Our Lives," in *Weavings* (Jan-Feb, 1987), 6-17
6. Ibid., 10.
7. Ibid., 11.
8. Eberhard Jüengel, *Justification: The Heart of the Christian Faith* (Edinburgh and New York: T & T Clark, 2001), 259.
9. Joseph Sittler, *Gravity and Grace* (Minneapolis: Augsburg Fortress, 2005), 3.

Chapter 3: Called to Life

1. James Nestingen, "Justification, Vocation, and Location in Luther's Reformation," in *Living Out Our Callings at Home* (St. Paul: Centered Life, 2003), 14.
2. Quoted in D. Michael Bennethum, *Listen! God Is Calling! Luther Speaks of Vocation, Faith, and Work* (Minneapolis: Augsburg Fortress, 2003), 66.
3. For further discussion of these four domains, see Robert Benne, *Ordinary Saints: An Introduction to the Christian Life* (Minneapolis: Fortress Press, 2003), Part III.
4. Paul Minus, *Taking Faith to Work* (St. Paul: Centered Life, 2004), 9.
5. Laura Nash and Scotty McLennan, *Church on Sunday, Work on Monday: The Challenge of Fusing Christian Values with Business Life* (San Francisco: Jossey-Bass, 2001), 4.
6. Frederick Buechner, *Wishful Thinking: A Theological ABC* (New York: Harper & Row, 1973), 95.
7. Nestingen, 12.
8. Minus, 25.
9. Nestingen, "Households As Masks of God: Going Home in Repentance and Faith" in *Living Out Our Callings at Home*, 20.
10. Elizabeth O'Connor, *Cry Pain, Cry Hope* (Waco, Tex.: Word, 1987), 14.
11. Parker Palmer, *Let Your Life Speak: Listening for the Voice of Vocation* (San Francisco: Jossey-Bass, 2000), 4-5.
12. Dennis Linn, Sheila Fabricant Linn, Matthew Linn, *Healing the Purpose of Your Life* (New York: Paulist Press, 1999), 9.
13. Gregory S. Clapper, *Living Your Heart's Desire: God's Call and Your Vocation* (Nashville: Upper Room Books, 2005), 13.

Chapter 4. Set Free to Work with God

1. *Lutheran Book of Worship* (Minneapolis: Augsburg, 1978), 56.
2. Michel Quoist, *The Meaning of Success* (Notre Dame, Ind.: Fides, 1963), 97.
3. Rochelle Melander and Harold Eppley, *Our Lives Are Not Our Own* (Minneapolis: Augsburg Fortress, 2003), 15.
4. Darrell Jodock, quoted in Mark Hanson, *Faithful and Courageous* (Minneapolis: Augsburg Fortress, 2005), 73.
5. Bennethum, 83.
6. *Martin Luther's Basic Writings*, (Minneapolis: Fortress Press, 2005), 596.

7. Richard Bolles, *How to Find Your Mission in the World* (San Francisco: Ten Speed Press, 1991, 2000), 49.

8. www.centeredlife.org.

9. Ibid.

Chapter 5: Finding Nurture and Support for Your Callings in Life

1. The two drawings are a response to the work of Dick Broholm and John Hoffman, *Developing Laity for Their Full Ministry* (Boston: The Center for the Ministry of the Laity, 1985).

2. Richard H. Bliese, "A Small Church Redefines Its Mission" *The Christian Century* (July 12, 2003), 24-27.

3. Bliese in "A Heart for Mission," *The Story* (Summer 2005), 8.

4. Martha R. Storz, *A World According to God: Practices for Putting Faith at the Center of Your Life* (San Francisco: Jossey-Bass, 2004), 10.

5. Charles Whiston, *Prayer* (Grand Rapids, Mich.: Eerdmans, 1972), 62, adapted.

6. Kolden, 38.

7. Quoted in Ron Klug, *How to Keep a Spiritual Journal* (Minneapolis: Augsburg Books, 2002), 9.

8. Hanson, *Faithful Yet Changing*, 38.

9. Dietrich Bonhoeffer, *Life Together: Prayerbook of the Bible* (Minneapolis: Fortress Press, 1996), 83.

10. Martin Luther, in *What Luther Says,* vol.1, Ewald Plass, ed. (St. Louis: Concordia, 1987), 235.

11. *Lutheran Book of Worship,* 53.

Recommended Reading

The Centered Life

Benne, Robert. *Ordinary Saints: An Introduction to the Christian Life.* Minneapolis: Fortress Press, 2003.

Bennethum, D. Michael. *Listen! God Is Calling! Luther Speaks of Vocation, Faith, and Work.* Minneapolis: Augsburg Fortress, 2003.

Bolles, Richard N. *How to Find Your Mission in Life.* Berkeley: Ten Speed Press, 1991, 2000.

Kelley, Geoffrey B. *Liberating Faith: Bonhoeffer's Message for Today.* Minneapolis: Augsburg Fortress, 1984.

Kolden, Marc. *The Christian's Calling in the World*. St. Paul: Centered Life, 2002.

Melander, Rochelle and Harold Eppley, *Our Lives Are Not Our Own: Saying "Yes" to God*. Minneapolis: Augsburg Fortress, 2003.

Palmer, Parker J. *Let Your Life Speak: Listening for the Voice of Vocation*. San Francisco: Jossey-Bass, 2000.

Work

Bliese, Richard; Miller, David W.; Moyet, Pamela J. *Living Out Our Callings in the Workplace*. St. Paul: Centered Life, 2004.

Minus, Paul. *Taking Faith to Work: Next Steps for Christian Discipleship*. St. Paul: Centered Life, 2004.

Family

Garland, Diana. *Sacred Stories of Ordinary Families: Living the Faith in Daily Life*. San Francisco: Jossey-Bass, 2003.

Nestingen, James; Garland, Diana; Martinson, Roland. *Living Out Our Callings at Home*. St. Paul: Centered Life, 2003.

Nilsen Family. *For Everything a Season: 75 Blessings for Daily Life*. Des Moines: Zion, 1999.

Spiritual Practices

Bass, Dorothy C., ed. *Practicing Our Faith: A Way of Life for Searching People*. San Francisco: Jossey-Bass, 1997.

Klug, Ron. *How to Keep a Spiritual Journal*. Minneapolis: Augsburg Books, 2002.

Postema, Don. *Space for God: The Study and Practice of Prayer and Spirituality*. Grand Rapids, Mich.: CRC Publications, 1983, 1997.

Storz, Martha Ellen. *A World According to God: Practices for Putting Faith at the Center of Your Life*. San Francisco: Jossey-Bass, 2004.

Acknowledgments

My sincere thanks to the following:

David Tiede, former president of Luther Seminary, who has always faithfully supported my work.

Richard Bliese, current president of Luther Seminary, for his encouragement and for writing the foreword to this book.

Ron Klug, my conversation partner, whose insights and inspiration were formative for the book.

Sally Peters for her partnership with me in developing the Centered Life Initiative.

Barb Gaiser for her helpful and tireless advice and counsel.

Jason Misselt for his perceptive reading of the manuscript.

Dick Broholm, close friend and mentor, whose vision and work has been a primary inspiration to me.

All my colleagues at the Center for Lifelong Learning at Luther Seminary for their faith and hard work.

Beth Lewis and Bill Huff of Augsburg Fortress, Publishers, for their encouragement and support.

All the friends who shared their stories with me. The stories are true, although some details were changed to protect privacy.

For more information on the Centered Life Initiative: www.centeredlife.org